The Sporting Life *Guide to*

YOUR HORSE

A VETERINARY BOOK

By Peter Rossdale

© 1993 Peter Rossdale

Published by The Sporting Life
Orbit House, 1 New Fetter Lane, London EC4A 1AR

First edition 1967
New edition, revised and updated, 1993

ISBN 0 901091 51 0

Cover origination by Reprosharp Ltd, London EC1
Text typeset by R&W Publications Ltd, Newmarket
Cover printed by Ark Litho, London SW19
Text printed and bound by The Bath Press, Bath

Acknowledgements
The author would like to acknowledge Rachel Leeks
and David Bennett for their help in producing this book.
Figures have also been reproduced from 'The Horse's Health
from A-Z' with kind permission of David & Charles

Cover
'Pebbles', Newmarket 1985. Photo: George Selwyn

Preface

This book contains articles contributed by the author and published weekly in *The Sporting Life* under the pseudonym of Veterinary Correspondent from 1965 to 1968. The articles were first published in book form in 1967. The series was initiated by the Editor, Ossie Fletcher, and Advertisement Manager, Alan Biggar. Assistance was provided by Sue Wreford who was co-editor with Peter Rossdale of 'The Horse's Health from A to Z'

The first edition has now been updated and brought into line with developments of the last 25 years. The original intention of the articles remains in the current edition, namely to inform horse owners and others with an interest in the horse of some of the ailments from which horses may suffer. The text is intended to be as non-technical as possible without losing accuracy.

Contents

1: The modern thoroughbred

Good horses which fail to remain sound are always a particularly bitter disappointment to those connected with them. During each flat racing season it is commonplace to hear of horses fancied for important races having to be withdrawn before the appointed day because they are difficult to train or unsound in one of their limbs. This is hardly surprising. The horse's limbs have become so specialised to serve the endpoint of speed that it is virtually standing on two middle fingers and two middle toes.

During the course of evolution, the horse has developed its body structure to serve two aims: the perfection of the mechanism for obtaining food and the attainment of speed. Speed is the principal means of defence in an animal which instinctively turns and runs away at the approach of danger. This specialisation for speed is reflected in the perfect symmetry of form of the head, neck and body. The long slender limbs support a relatively heavy body. The powerful muscles bunched at the shoulders and thighs transmit their power through the tendons to the feet, providing a mechanical effect of power and propulsion which has few equals in the animal kingdom.

There are tremendous forces exerted on the limbs by a galloping horse weighing perhaps 1,100 lbs and travelling at 40 mph. Such extreme specialisation renders the horse particularly liable to leg injuries and to this must be added the effect imposed by the weight of the rider on the normal equilibrium.

To understand the structures of a horse's limb, it is helpful to compare them with our own. Our wrist is equivalent to the horse's knee, and the term used for this joint in both species is the carpus. It is below the carpus that the most extreme degree of specialisation has occurred (Fig 1.1). In our own hand we have five bones which run from the wrist to the knuckles and are known as the metacarpal bones (Fig 1.2), but in the horse only the middle one of these bones is fully developed and functional. This is the cannon bone, the horse's fetlock joint being equivalent to our middle knuckle. The three bones which form our middle finger are found in the horse as the first two pastern bones and the pedal bone. The hoof, which surrounds all of the pedal bone and half of the pastern bone, may be compared with our own nails.

This tremendous lengthening in the bones of the forelimb and the reduction in the number of digits from five to one, results in a limb which is strong and relatively light. A comparable process of adaptation is seen in the hindlimb, the stifle being equivalent to the human knee joint and the hock to our ankle. Below the ankle the same elongation and reduction in the number of bones is seen as in the forelimb.

The evolution of the limbs of the horse and the reduction in the number of bones has been studied from fossils which have been found in many parts of the world. One of the earliest horses was a four-toed horse called Eohippus (Fig 1.3a)

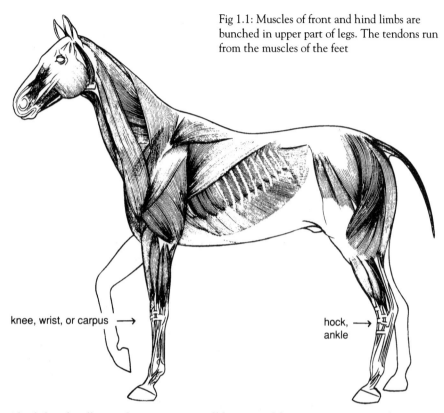

Fig 1.1: Muscles of front and hind limbs are bunched in upper part of legs. The tendons run from the muscles of the feet

knee, wrist, or carpus ⟶

hock, ⟶
ankle

which lived millions of years ago, a small but graceful creature averaging about 12in in height at the withers. The forelimb bore four complete 'fingers', each ending in a hoof-like nail, whereas the hind limb ended in three toes.

Later development in the horse resulted in the form known as Mesohippus which was roughly the size of a wolf, up to 24in high (6 hands). The fourth toes of the forelimb had by this time disappeared (Fig 1.3b) and both the hands and the feet had three 'digits' only, the middle one in each case being much the largest and bearing the majority of the weight. Still later in evolution we find the first one-toed horse (Fig 1.3c) known as Pliohippus which was some 40in (10 hands) high.

The modern horse stands on one toe only (Fig 1.3d) but the remnants of the other toes can still be seen in the splint bones which are found on either sides of the cannon bone. Below the knee and the hock there are no muscles, only tendons. These tendons form two groups: those which pull the limbs forward, known as extensors, and those which pull them back, known as flexors. The tendons are surrounded by sheaths containing tendon oil which helps to lubricate the movement of the tendons as the muscles exert their pull.

There are two ligaments (see diagram on page 17) which help to prevent the

The modern thoroughbred

limb from being over-extended. One is the suspensory ligament which runs from the back of the knee (or hock in the hind limb) to the fetlock joint, and then sends two branches to the front of the foot. The other is the check ligament which also starts at the back of the knee and is attached to the deep flexor tendon. The muscles, tendons and joints act as a series of pulleys and levers. Moving in perfect unison, they propel the body forward.

The whole system of the limb provides not only a driving force, but a cushion against the concussion that is felt when the foot strikes the ground. It is small

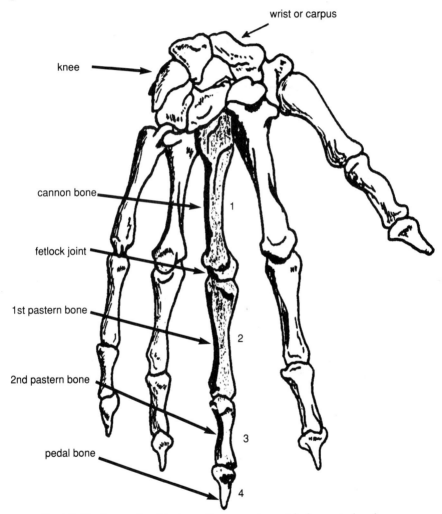

Fig 1.2: The human hand is shown for comparison with the equivalent bones marked 1 to 4. The small bones of the wrist are also shown

wonder that this highly complicated system is prone to injury. When we speak of injuries in this connection, we mean not only bruises or cuts, but also sprains of the tendons, pulled muscles, fractures, inflammation of the joints and tearing of ligaments. Some of these injuries are particularly liable to recur, especially if the horse is exercised before recovery. It is clear that the term 'difficult to train' is particularly applicable to unsoundness of the limbs.

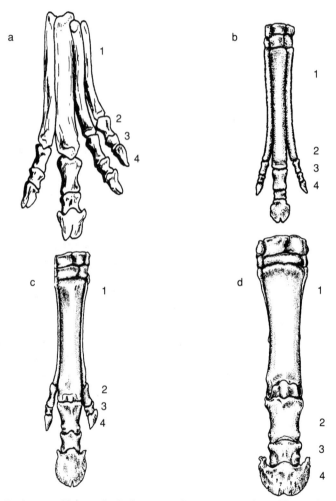

Fig 1.3: Evolution of horse's limb showing reduction in number of bones from (a) earliest known types (eohippus) which lived many millions of years ago, to (d) the modern horse's foot. The number of toes has been reduced from four to one. In the diagram of the modern horse's foot, the cannon bone is numbered 1, and is shown with the splint bones on either side. The pastern bones are numbered 2 and 3 and pedal bone 4. *Not to scale*

The modern thoroughbred

2: The feet

The horse's foot is a very good example of the wonderful way in which different parts of the body become adapted in the course of evolution to meet a particular purpose. In the development of limbs thus specialised for speed, we find that the propulsive force exerted by the muscles through those limbs is capable of propelling a half-ton weight of horse at great speeds over long distances. Whether the horse is walking or galloping these forces act entirely through the single toes of the four feet. In consequence, the feet are required to meet considerable wear and tear from all kinds of surfaces.

The feet form an important part of the anti-concussion mechanism of the limbs. They protect the body from severe jolts, enabling the horse to move smoothly and rhythmically in motion. Lightness and toughness are the essential qualities of the horse's foot. It is built around the most distant bone of the limb, equivalent to the final bone in our middle finger.

The internal structures of the foot are protected by the stout outer casing of horn which may be likened to our own nails. This horn grows at a steady rate, continually replacing loss by wear and tear. The frog and bulbs of the heel act as a kind of shock absorber when the foot meets the ground, as well as forming additional protection to the foot itself.

The conformation of the horse's foot is very important, as might be expected from a part which is most of the time in active use. The requirements of a good foot are that it should be of the right size to 'house' its internal structures comfortably, the correct shape to meet the specialised functions of weight bearing and shock-absorbing. The weight of the horse should be carried on only a portion of the foot, the bearing surface of the wall and a small area of adjacent sole, the 'bars' (which are in reality continuations of the wall) and the frog (Fig 2.1). Any shape of foot that results in an unequal or unnatural distribution of weight on these structures may affect soundness. Thus, the foot with a flat rather than vaulted sole and one with low, unprotected heels will be prone to bruising. The upright, narrow foot may eliminate the normal frog pressure and thus interfere with its shock-absorbing function.

The angle of slope of the foot is also important as it may affect the degree of stress imposed upon the back tendons (the deep one of which arises from the foot) and upon the coffin joint, due to the effect upon the angle of the bones forming it. The ideal slope of the foot is one where the line of the pastern and the foot is continuous (Fig 2.2). In the forefoot this is usually about 50°, in the hindfoot 55°.

It is interesting to note the differences between the shape of the fore and hind feet, the former being adapted to the greater degree of concussion that it experiences. Unfortunately, nature did not foresee the uses to which man would put the horse, nor the type of surfaces on which it would be asked to perform them. Because of this, it has become necessary that the horse should be shod with

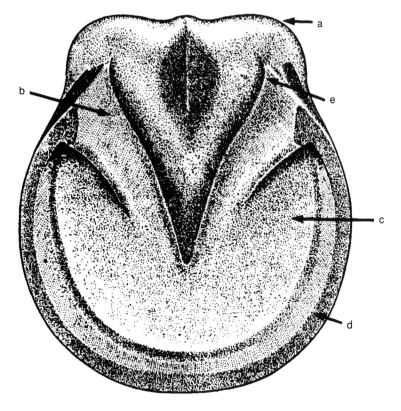

Fig 2.1: Horse's foot (a) bulb of heel, (b) bar, (c) horny sole, (d) bearing surface of wall, and (e) frog

a shoe which, by virtue of its especially hard-wearing character, is also rigid and prevents normal expansion and contraction of the heels. Although good trimming and shoeing can go a long way towards overcoming some of the defects of badly shaped feet, it is also true that poor trimming and faulty shoeing often robs a good foot of its normal functions. Uneven or unnatural distribution of weight upon the bearing surfaces of the foot may cause damage to the joints, tendons, ligaments and bones further up the limb.

Conditions of the foot are a common source of lameness. For the convenience of description these may be described under the different terms or headings which are in everyday use. It must be remembered, however, that the different parts of the foot are so closely associated with one another that often the disease or injury to one part leads directly to untoward damage in another.

When an abscess forms between the horn and the coffin or pedal bone, it will cause very acute pain. The pus has very little chance of escaping and there is, therefore, considerable pressure on the sensitive parts. Abscesses are usually found in the sole of the foot, but the pus may track upwards beneath the horn towards the coronet or the bulbs of the heel, where it eventually bursts out. An abscess will heal more readily if drained at the lowest point, and therefore it is always important to cut the horn beneath the abscess so that it drains from the sole. Once the pus is allowed to escape in this way, the animal is soon relieved of pain and healing follows quite rapidly. It is usually necessary to put some form of plug or covering over the hole that has been made, so that grit does not work its way through the opening in the horn.

Nails and other sharp objects are a common source of injury to the sole of the foot and penetration may cause damage to the bone itself, depending on the site of entry, as well as allowing infection to enter with abscess formation. The coffin bone (Fig 2.2) is in a position of vulnerability to damage from a penetrating wound in the front half of the foot. Cracks in the wall of the hoof, or sand cracks as they are often called, may be very troublesome, especially if they extend into the coronary band which is the seat of growth of the horn.

A condition which is not so commonly met in thoroughbreds today and which is possibly more prevalent in heavier breeds and ponies, is one known as 'laminitis'. Literally this means inflammation of the structures between the pedal bone and the hoof. The pedal bone is covered by a velvet-like membrane which nourishes the horn and by interlocking with it, helps to keep the bone in position. This membrane is heavily supplied by blood vessels and when the circulation is upset inflammation results, causing great pain. More than one foot may be affected at the same time and the horse has great difficulty in standing in a comfortable position. In an attempt to ease the weight off its feet it will adopt unusual positions, such as bunching all four feet together beneath it, or stretching them as far in front or behind as possible. It will be very reluctant to move if asked to do so and it may be difficult or impossible to lift any one of the limbs. The foot will feel very hot due to

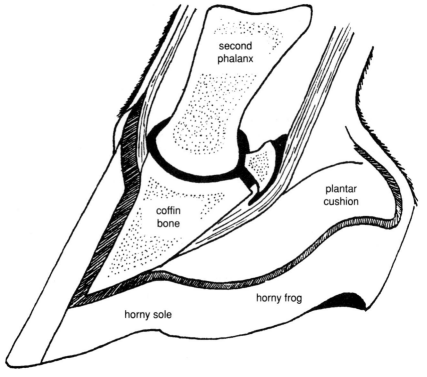

Fig 2.2: Position of coffin (pedal) bone in relation to sole

the disturbance of the blood supply.

The causes of laminitis are not always known, although they are likely to follow any toxic condition or digestive upset. When one considers the relatively great distance of the horse's foot from the heart, it is perhaps remarkable that disturbances of the circulation in the foot are not found more commonly. One of the results of laminitis is that the support given to the front of the coffin bone by the velvet-like membrane is considerably reduced. The point of the coffin bone then drops and may eventually come through the sole of the foot.

The foot contains a joint formed by the second phalanx, the coffin bone and the navicular bone. The deep flexor tendon runs over the navicular bone. Inflammation of the navicular bone is much more common in horses over the age of 7 years. The bone itself may become diseased and ulcerated at the point where the tendon passes over it. This causes pain and the animal goes unsound. Navicular disease nearly always affects the front legs and the horse stands with the affected limb placed in a forward position, often described as 'pointing'. If both forelimbs are affected, it may continually change its position, pointing first one then the other

The feet

foreleg. It is a feature of the condition that, in the early stages, the lameness will often get better or disappear with exercise.

One of the bones of the foot may be fractured. X-ray examination is necessary to make a diagnosis of a fracture and distinguish the condition from the much more common one of an abscess.

Inflammation of the coffin bone is also a source of lameness and is another case where X-ray examination is helpful for diagnosis. Injury to the structures associated with the coffin joint may lead to a soft filling which can be felt at the coronet. If the membrane lining the coffin bone and which nourishes the horn becomes inflamed for any reason, it may affect the horn. This becomes dry and brittle, a condition often referred to as 'seedy toe'.

Another condition seen more commonly in the heavy breeds is one known as 'sidebones'. It gets its name from the fact that the 'springy' cartilage on either side of the heels becomes hard and bony due to injuries. When this happens, it interferes with the shock absorbing mechanism of the foot and the animal may go lame.

A club foot is one where the angle of the foot is very steep. This generally reflects the shape of the coffin bone which is inclined to be U-shaped in this condition. Club foot appears to be an inherited condition. It does not always affect the soundness of a horse, but it may result in changes further up the limb in a similar manner to other badly-shaped feet.

3: *The tendons*

Sprained or 'bowed' tendons have probably caused the premature retirement of more horses from racing, both on the flat and over jumps, than any other injury or abnormality. In order to understand the reasons for the change that takes place in a tendon when it is injured it is necessary to know something about its function and normal structure.

A tendon is a tough band of specialised fibrous tissue arising from a muscle at one end and attached to a bone at the other. It is through the tendons that the muscles act upon the bones. The strength of a tendon is based on a complicated, yet orderly, system of closely packed strands of tissue known as collagen fibres. The fibres have a hierarchical arrangement of bundles embedded in a cement-like substance known as a matrix.The bundles are further grouped into collections known as a fascicle. The fibres have a wavy or crimped course which produces an undulating structure that exists throughout the tendon length and provides the tendon with some ability to be stretched. Although there are tendons associated with most muscles of the body, those that are commonly injured in the horse are the flexor tendons, particularly the superficial flexor tendon, situated behind the cannon bone of the foreleg (Fig 3.1).

We have already seen that in the horse, given its specialisation for speed, the muscle masses are found in the upper parts of the limb only. Thus the tendons under consideration, although attached to bones below the fetlock joint, arise from muscles in the forearm. In addition to their prime function, these tendons, together with the check and the suspensory ligaments, act as part of the 'support' apparatus of the fetlock and the lower leg. The suspensory is, in reality, a tendon, but having lost its muscle during the process of evolution, is now attached to bone at both ends and classed as a ligament.

The body weight of the horse is carried largely on the forehand, resulting in considerable stress on the forelegs at fast paces. It is for this reason that sprains, the commonest of all injuries to tendons, are encountered in the forelimbs rather than the hind limbs. Sprain of a tendon almost invariably occurs when the horse is galloping. The tone and elasticity of healthy, fit muscles enable them to respond smoothly to the demands of the pace and to maintain an efficient buffer system against concussion on the skeleton. But, as muscles tire, they lose much of their natural elasticity and more and more strain is thereby thrown upon the tendons. Indeed, it might almost be said that a sprained tendon is the end result of muscle fatigue. We rarely hear of a horse 'breaking down' in the early part of a race, but rather in the final stages when tiring and under pressure.

A sprain may involve either or both of the flexor tendons at any level between the knees and the fetlock, or the structures forming the stay apparatus (that is, the check or suspensory ligaments). Clinically, all the signs of inflammation (heat, pain and swelling) rapidly develop in the injured structure, the degree of inflammation depending on the severity of the injury. Although injury to a tendon can readily be detected, the exact nature of the injury is often extremely difficult to assess. Post mortem examinations of cases which, before death, appeared to be typical sprains may reveal the damage and inflammation to be confined to the tissues surrounding the tendon and not within the tendon itself.

When a true sprain occurs, however, a variable number of the tendon fibres are ruptured, and blood and inflammatory fluid rapidly collect in the area, resulting in the whole tendon becoming thickened. The connective tissue between the bundles of fibres becomes swamped with inflammatory fluid which results in bundles of normal fibres becoming widely separated. This 'forcing apart' of the intact bundles of fibres further destroys the normal structure of the tendon and increases its weakness.

During repair, three disadvantageous events occur. The first is that the fibrous material laid down is immature and tends, therefore, to bleed and rupture more easily than the original structures of the tendon present prior to the injury. Secondly, the new fibres are organised at random rather than in an orderly fashion. Thirdly, the crimping pattern is lost and hence there is a reduction in the elasticity of the tendon resulting in a greater risk of its tearing once again at the point of healing or in the tendon above or below the position of the scar. In summary, the damage is repaired gradually by the laying down of unspecialised fibrous tissue which lacks both the

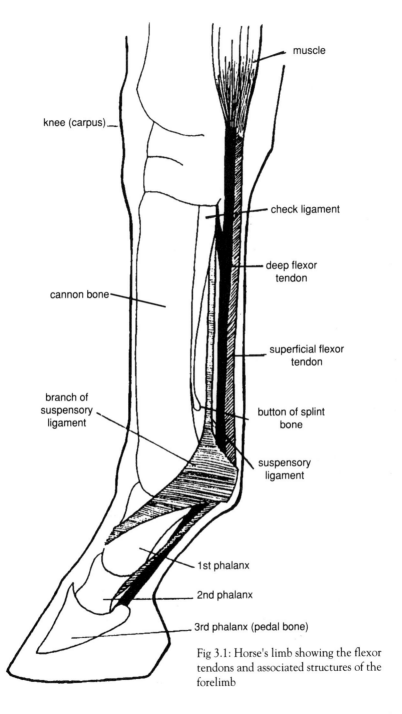

muscle

knee (carpus)

check ligament

deep flexor tendon

cannon bone

superficial flexor tendon

branch of suspensory ligament

button of splint bone

suspensory ligament

1st phalanx

2nd phalanx

3rd phalanx (pedal bone)

Fig 3.1: Horse's limb showing the flexor tendons and associated structures of the forelimb

The tendons

17

tensile strength and bundle conformation of the healthy tendon tissue and is a poor apology for the original.

In cases where the majority of the damage is on the exterior of the tendon, and also where the internal sprain is severe, a considerable amount of inflammatory fluid collects around the tendon and this rapidly causes adhesions between the injured tendon and adjacent structures. When the horse is eventually returned to training these adhesions may tear under the stress of galloping and will result in a renewal of the inflammatory reaction in the leg. Many a horse that appears to have broken down a second time after returning to training following a long rest is, in fact, suffering from the effects of torn adhesions. The treatment of sprained tendons poses one of the most difficult problems for those engaged in equine practice. This is hardly surprising when we know that a tendon, once destroyed, is never completely restored. Whatever form of treatment is undertaken, all specialists agree that the earlier the therapy is instituted, which inevitably includes some degree of rest from strenuous exercise, the better. Injuries tend to be progressive and one of the most important means of overcoming them is to identify their presence as early as possible in the course of development.

Until recently, the methods of detection employed have been the traditional ones of observation and feeling for enlargement and heat. The expert trainer or stable hand can often identify a change at the earliest stage of injury. However, many horses suffering from an early sprain may be rested for an insufficient period and the injury becomes exacerbated through exercise or, even, through being made to gallop at racing pace. The introduction of ultrasound scanning has made the diagnosis of tendon injury much more accurate over the last five years or so. It is now possible to look into and identify the presence of damage to the tendon fibres.

The aims of treatment in the early stages are to reduce the amount of haemorrhage and inflammatory fluid that collects within and around the injured tendon. The normal methods of reducing and controlling inflammation are applicable, except that the urgency of such treatment is much greater in the case of a sprained tendon.

The swelling and bowing of sprained tendons can largely be prevented by pressure and cold applications if these are applied soon enough. Once again, the use of anti-inflammatory drugs combined with pressure bandaging has greatly facilitated the early treatment of these cases. Where the sprain is only very slight, the treatment may appear to be so effective that the trainer is tempted to return the horse to work within a very short time. Unfortunately, however, only the symptoms have been treated and the original injury remains. If the horse is returned to training at this stage, the leg will invariably blow up again.

We all know that most horses that have suffered tendon sprain disappear from the racing scene for a very long time. The rate of healing of any tissue is largely dependent on its blood supply, whichin the tendon is somewhat poor, so that healing tends to be slow. Firing and blistering which were once commonly used in an attempt to increase blood flow have largely been discarded in favour of more modern therapies. Both these procedures are now considered not to be in the best interest of the welfare of the horse. As to the efficacy of firing, the veterinary profession has abandoned this approach in favour of other methods.

The most recent approach, largely pioneered by Dr Larry Bramlage of Ohio State University, USA, is to sever the superior check ligament. This is attached on to the forearm and then directly onto the superficial flexor tendon. It forms part of the stay apparatus which prevents the fetlock from being overextended when a horse gets tired or makes a particularly forceful landing on the foreleg. The object of the surgery is to relieve the extreme tension that may build up in these circumstances on the superficial flexor tendon. It therefore allows for better healing and less risk of recurrence of an injury. The success of this surgery is not, as one might expect, 100 per cent but, if performed early enough in the development of an injury, it is probably the most effective and logical of all therapies so far devised for this debilitating injury.

There are constant attempts to find more efficient methods of promoting increased circulation within damaged tendons. These include deep-heat therapy, irradiation, injections of various substances and surgery upon the tendons themselves. Not surprisingly, the results of the treatments are not conclusive, especially in view of the difficulty of accurate diagnosis of the degree of injury in each case.

Whatever treatment is used, some rest is essential. This may mean the horse being restricted to a loose box or given walking exercise. The period of rest necessary may range from 3 months to 1-2 years, depending on the amount of damage to the tendon at the start of treatment. In many cases, especially where the damage is severe, complete healing never occurs and the horse is no longer useful for athletic performance. Ultrasound scanning helps considerably in assessing the outcome of treatment and the time at which it is safe to put the horse back into training.

4: *The splint bones*

There are a number of commonly used terms which, while giving some idea of the condition in question, are an impediment to a true appreciation of the scientific principles involved. To name a few which have been in use for many years: 'splints', 'sore shins', 'curbs', 'joints', 'bowed tendons' and 'bog spavins'. Without real understanding of what is happening to the structures of the body in each of these cases, it is difficult both for the veterinary surgeon and for the trainer or owner to follow a correct course of treatment.

When a horse is said to have a 'splint' most people know that it is an enlargement or lump on the inside or outside of one of the cannon bones, usually of the forelimbs. The splint bones, as we have seen, are thin, slender bones, one of which runs down each side of the cannon bone. These bones serve no real purpose, but are remnants of the extra digits which the horse has lost during the course of evolution. They are closely attached to the main cannon bone by a very fine ligament. The upper part of the bone is called the head, which is connected to the button at the lower end by the thin slender shaft (Fig 4.1). The term 'splint' signifies an enlargement close to the position of the splint bone. There are, however, a number of different causes of such enlargements, each of which requires a different treatment. That is why 'splint' is not a particularly helpful term.

In Fig 4.1, three different types of splints are illustrated. In one case there is a fracture of the shaft. This results in the formation of a callus which is the body's normal reaction in the repair of fractures. The callus is new bone which unites the two fractured ends.

On the right upper part of the figure, a second type of 'splint' is shown. Here the ligament which binds the splint bone to the cannon bone has become inflamed and the reaction has produced a fibrous enlargement which may well be painful to the touch. Below, a swelling is shown which is a result of a reaction on the surface of the splint bone or the cannon bone. These swellings result from inflammation of the outer lining of the bone itself. The cause of these enlargements may be concussion, which is why they are more common in the fore than the hind limbs. In the young animal the ligament binding the splint bone to the cannon bone allows relatively more movement of the splint bone than in the older animal. As the animal becomes older, bone is laid down and replaces the ligament so that the splint bone becomes fixed to the cannon, preventing this movement. It is the very slight movement when the animal moves that tends to cause inflammation in the ligament, and we would therefore expect to find this type of enlargement as the most common form in foals and yearlings.

Fractures may occur at any age, as the result of blows as well as of concussion. Splints are found more often on the inside of the limb than on the outer aspect. This is due to the fact that this side of the limb probably receives more concussion by virtue of the conformation and anatomy of the limb. There is also more

Fig 4.1: View from behind cannon bone (a) head of splint bone, (b) ligament binding splint to cannon bone, (c) shaft of splint bone, (d) fracture of shaft with callus, (e) button of splint bone, (f) reaction round splint due to inflammation in ligament, (g) reaction of surface lining of splint and cannon bone

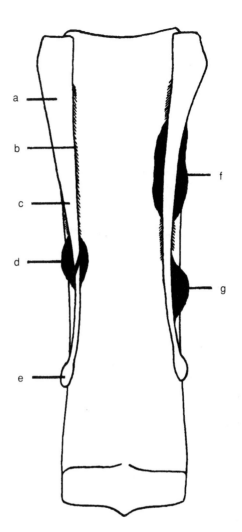

likelihood of a blow from the opposite limb.

It is only by an X-ray examination of the limb that we can differentiate between these different types of enlargements. Further, it is only when we have done this that we can be rational about the treatment and assess the outlook in each particular case. The fracture requires rest for at least six weeks. During that time a supporting bandage is helpful. If healing still does not take place, surgical removal of part of the bone may be necessary. Inflammation of the ligament will probably subside with rest alone, although it may be necessary to administer drugs either locally or in general form to reduce the amount of inflammation present. If the reaction is such that new bone is being formed at an increasing rate, steps may be

The splint bones

taken to stop this by irradiating the area with radioactive substances.

When the ligament is the seat of trouble there may be very little swelling to see, although the horse goes lame. Eventually, if we continue to work the horse, the reaction may become so great that a swelling will appear and the cause of the original lameness will then be obvious. An X-ray examination in the early stages can, however, be used to make a diagnosis of the lameness.

Although blistering and firing were traditional treatments for these conditions, a combination of box rest and non-steroidal anti-inflammatory drugs (NSAID) such as phenylbutazone are now normally prescribed. Placing the area in a magnetic current (blue boot treatment) and cold water therapy are other means of reducing inflammation and encouraging a callus to form where an actual fracture is present. (A callus is the name given to new bone which bridges the ends of a fracture, thereby stabilising the two ends and allowing a proper union to take place in repair).

Besides lameness arising from the pain, serious damage may be caused if the enlargement presses into the suspensory ligament or tendons which run down the back of the limb. In each case the swellings may be temporary or permanent, depending on how much new bone is formed, either as a result of the callus or of the reaction to the surface lining of the bone. Many of the reactions which can be seen as prominent swellings are purely soft fibrous tissue and will be eliminated by the body in the course of time. If new bone is formed, however, this will not occur and a permanent enlargement will result.

Splints may also be referred to as being active, which means that they are still growing in size and the irritation that produces them is still present. Again, it is only by an X-ray examination that we can be sure whether or not the splint is active.

Bad conformation is likely to give rise to any of the types of splints that have been described. This applies especially to conformation below the fetlock joint. If the foot is of a bad shape or the toe points at too great an angle to the midline, it is probable that there will be an uneven distribution of weight when the forelimb meets the ground. This is particularly common in young animals where the bone is immature. When a yearling has faulty conformation in his forelimbs, it is not surprising that an enlargement will often be found at the seat of splint.

The great importance of care of the feet at all stages of a horse's development, has already been emphasised and splints once again illustrate the point.

5: *The sore shin*

'Sore shins' or 'bucked shins' are often used terms in the racing stable, the shin being the front of the cannon. The outer lining of the bone or periosteum becomes torn and inflamed due, occasionally, to a blow, but more commonly to galloping on firm going. As in the case of the splint, pain and swelling result. Initially the swelling is due to inflammatory fluid collecting between the outer lining of the bone and the bone itself. At this stage it may be dispersed successfully with treatment (Fig 5.1). Later, as first fibrous tissue and then new bone is laid down, the enlargement becomes permanent. Some cases of persistent sore shins are caused by a minute hair-line fracture in the bone casing (known as stress fracture) which may possibly be diagnosed by X-ray examination. The enlargement in these cases is due to callus formation at the site of fracture.

In recent years, the technique of scintigraphy has provided a more accurate means of diagnosing bony inflammation, including stress fractures. Scintigraphy involves injecting a very weak radioactive substance into the horse's bloodstream. This becomes targeted on bone and accumulates in greater concentration where the bone is inflamed. A picture may then be computed using a geiger counter to measure the amount of radioactivity.

Sore shins are most commonly met in two-year-olds, especially during the first part of the season when they are being put into fast work for the first time. Older horses, however, may also suffer from the condition when they are brought back into work after being laid off, or when the ground is particularly hard.

Anti-inflammatory drugs, cold applications, blisters and the firing iron are methods variously employed to treat sore shins, depending largely on the severity and duration of the condition. However, where the lameness is due to a stress fracture, a period of rest is imperative to avoid constant recurrence of the symptoms. In most cases, however, it is possible to return a horse to full training after a minimum period of light work.

Any swelling on the back of the hock is usually referred to as a curb and the area affected is known as the 'seat of curb'. A true curb is caused by a sprain of one of the ligaments in this area, the resultant inflammation and swelling producing a bulge in the overlying tendon. This can be seen as a break in the normal straight line when the hock is viewed from the side. Any conformation of this joint that imposes an increased strain on the ligaments at the back of the hock will increase the likelihood of curbs. Hence, we hear people speak of 'curby or sickle-hocks'. Not in all cases, however, is an enlargement at the seat of curb a true curb. In some horses, the head of the lateral splint bone may cause a projection at this site. This is known as a 'false curb' and is not detrimental to the horse's action.

We often hear a trainer talk of a horse having a 'joint'. By this he means that there is pain and swelling present in the region of the fetlock. This is probably one of the vaguest terms in common use, covering many conditions involving several

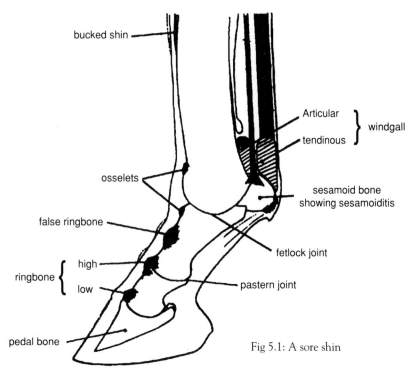

bucked shin

Articular } windgall

tendinous }

osselets

false ringbone

sesamoid bone
showing sesamoiditis

ringbone { high
low

fetlock joint

pastern joint

pedal bone

Fig 5.1: A sore shin

separate structures. The injury may be within the joint, resulting in an arthritis of varying degree, or around the joint involving the ligaments themselves and the bones at the points of attachment of these ligaments. One common example of the latter injury is known as sesamoiditis, an inflammation of the two small bones situated behind the fetlock joint.

'Osselets' (a term commonly used in America) are bone growths developing as a result of ligaments tearing at their attachments on the pastern and shin bones bordering the fetlock joint. More specific terms have been used widely and recognised by horsemen for years to describe conditions associated with particular joints and tendon sheaths. As these terms have been coined to describe the clinical appearance of the abnormalities, they again fail to give any indication of the structures involved.

For instance, 'ring bone' is one such vague term which is applied to different conditions of the pastern bones, below the fetlock joint. Ring bone may be the result of a sprain of one of the ligaments of the pastern or pedal joints, an arthritis of one of these joints, or an inflammation of the bone itself. It is possibly a combination of all three and it is customary to classify it as high, low or false according to its position. As with other bony conditions, we can only make a diagnosis and give a view on the outcome of these swellings seen at the site of the

The sore shin

ring bone if an X-ray examination is made.

'Windgall' is a term used more frequently in the hunting than the racing stable to describe distension of the fetlock joint (articular windgall) or the tendon sheath in the same region (tendinous windgall). The swelling of the joint or sheath is merely a sign of underlying damage to these structures. Both the degree and type of injury must be investigated thoroughly before the significance of the windgall can be assessed.

'Spavin' is usually taken to indicate some disease of the hock joint or its adjacent structure. Bone spavin describes the formation of new bone over the inner aspect of the hock and is associated with arthritis of the joints between the small hock bones. Bog spavin denotes a filling of the hock joint itself.

It is thus apparent that behind many commonly used terms lie several different conditions. Before any attempt at treatment, the veterinary surgeon must necessarily establish what structures are involved and the degree of abnormality present.

6: *Joint stresses and arthritis*

A joint is a place where movement can occur between two or more sets of bones. No joint, however, is formed by bone meeting bone: the ends of the bones are covered by a layer of specialised cartilage which provides a smooth, gliding surface. Between the opposing cartilages is the joint cavity, filled with joint oil (or synovial fluid) and surrounded by the joint capsule, the outer layer of which is intimately associated with the ligaments of the joint and acts with these structures to prevent exaggerated movement, such as over extension or over flexion. The inner layer of the capsule secretes the joint oil which serves both as a lubricant and as source of nourishment to the articular cartilage.

Because the prime function of a joint is movement, lubrication is extremely important. It has been shown in man that even lightly working an unlubricated joint may result in the cartilage being worn down to the bone within a few hours. Normally there is a constant film of synovial fluid separating the joint surfaces, thus reducing wear of the cartilage to the minimum.

The mechanics of joint movement are complicated. It is sufficient to say here that the joint is a finer piece of engineering than anything devised by man. Unfortunately, a fault can occur in even the best of systems, and in the case of the joint, arthritis results.

Arthritis is a familiar term because of the human condition of rheumatoid arthritis. Arthritis literally means inflammation of the structures, such as bone and cartilage, forming the joint. Horses do not, in fact, suffer such inflammation but rather a degeneration of those tissues. The joint capsule may become inflamed and this represents a true arthritis. The more common condition affecting horses is what is now generally termed 'degenerative joint disease'. In this, the joint surface,

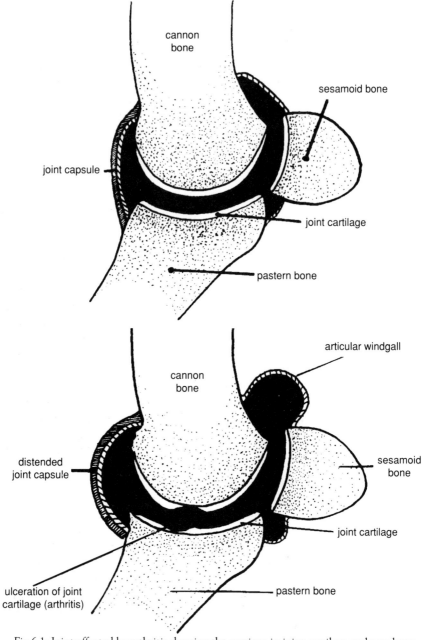

Fig 6.1: Joint affected by arthritis showing the erosions in joint cartilage and new bone formation as a 'spur' on the border of the pastern bone

Joint stresses and arthritis

composed of cartilage, loses its normal resilience and smooth surface leading to ulceration or erosion. This erosion of the cartilage may be superficial or penetrate deeply to affect the underlying bone.

The bone reacts by growing small projections or osteophytes (Fig 6.1). The osteophytes may break off and result in loose fragments in the joint. These may be described as 'joint mice'. The effects of the eroded surface of the joint are increased synovial fluid and consequent swelling of the joint which can be seen and felt readily on the outside. They also result in varying degrees of pain and, therefore, lameness.

OCD (osteochondrosis dissecans) is another condition of the joint surface. The cartilage at the surface, particularly in the hock and stifle joint, may become dry and the surface layers flaky. This is a condition particularly associated with young animals and may be associated with swelling of the joint, leading eventually to lameness.

Bone cysts are most commonly found in the femur and tibia of the hind limb and the shoulder joint of the forelimb, although they may occur in any bone at any age. It is not known how they develop but one theory is that a breach of the joint lining occurs and the pressure of the synovial fluid causes a duct to develop which penetrates into the bone beneath and results in a cyst or bone cavity.

It is usual to divide arthritis into two categories: infectious and non-infectious. An example of the former is 'joint ill' which, although a serious disease in the young foal, is seldom encountered in the horse in training. It is perhaps fortunate that the horse is prey to far fewer types of arthritis than humans, crippling joint diseases such as gout and rheumatoid arthritis being unknown in the horse. Most cases of degenerative joint disease in racehorses are due to injury or trauma and may be broadly grouped under the term 'traumatic arthritis'.

The healthy joint is quite capable of coping with the normal wear and tear of movement and weight bearing. However, when for any reason the stresses imposed upon the joints become excessive, damage is likely to occur. Degenerative joint disease in the racehorse is more commonly the result of continual stress imposed on the limbs by training and racing than of any single severe injury to the joints. The joints which are most likely to be affected are therefore those which are exposed to the greatest degree of stress, both of movement and weight bearing.

In man, who is upright amd whose weight is borne by a single pair of legs, the commonest site of arthritic changes are the hip and knee joints. In the horse, however, the forelimbs support the main bulk of the animal's weight, both at rest and in motion, and the joints which probably cause the most trouble while the animal is in training are the fetlock and knee, the latter being the equivalent of the wrist in the human. These joints are very much concerned with the cushioning of the concussion that is transmitted through the forelimbs during motion. At the same time, they are central parts of the leverage system which is provided by the forelimbs in the propulsion of the horse.

The tremendous thrust provided by a horse travelling at speed is absorbed at one phase of the gallop on a single foreleg. The stress imposed on the joints of this leg is very evident in action photographs in which the degree of 'over extension' of the knee and fetlock may be readily appreciated.

The skeleton of the horse is not fully mature until the animal is over four years old, yet many thoroughbreds are exposed to the great physical demands of racing when they are two year olds. It is hardly surprising, therefore, that many fall by the wayside due to some form of unsoundness. Degenerative joint disease, however, is a very much more serious problem, as many young horses are permanently handicapped by a chronic incurable arthritis at this early stage in their career. The changes taking place in a diseased joint are usually insidious in onset, commencing with a slight inflammation of the inner lining of the joint capsule and an increase in the quantity of synovial fluid, causing a slight distension of the joint. As the horse continues to work, the joint cartilage becomes ulcerated, thus breaking the continuity of the smooth surface. Unless the horse is rested at this stage, the condition of the joint continues to deteriorate. To compensate for the reduction in area of joint surface, due to the increasing area of cartilage erosion, outgrowths of first cartilage, and later bone, appear along the edges of the joint. At this stage the condition is often described as 'osteoarthritis'.

In a few cases, small fractured portions of the bony outgrowth are present as 'joint mice'. Such changes are irreversible and, while correct treatment and time may allow a percentage of these horses to race again satisfactorily, the affected joint never returns to its normal healthy stage. The amount of new bone that is formed around a joint depends in part upon the joint that is affected. In those where there is only a small amount of movement, nature attempts to immobilise the joint and thus prevent movement. Examples of this in the horse are true ring bone, involving the pastern, and a bone spavin, involving the small joints of the hock.

Although many horses may lose their 'action' during the earlier phases of degenerative joint disease, distinct lameness may not occur until advanced bony changes are present in the joint. Early diagnosis of the disease is thus of paramount importance. In some cases, abnormalities in the horse's action can be detected only during the first few minutes of exercise, in others only at slow paces. Two-year-olds with a history of 'warming up', moving badly at the trot, but becoming normal at the canter, are often suffering from early degenerative joint disease.

Examination of the affected joint will reveal an increase in the amount of synovial fluid, resulting in a distension of the joint capsule accompanied by the usual signs of inflammation - that is, heat and pain, the latter being provoked by manipulation of the joint. Before the veterinary surgeon can decide upon a line of treatment, however, he must ascertain the degree of damage within the joint and, for this, X-ray examination is essential. In addition, analysis of a sample of joint oil may prove a useful guide as changes in the joint are accompanied by changes in the composition of this fluid.

7: Treatment of joints

There is a constant search for more successful methods of treatment for the non-infective forms of degenerative joint disease in both man and animals. Unfortunately, the fact that the fundamental causes of many types of joint disease are not fully understood makes the approach to their treatment extremely difficult. Furthermore, once the structure of a joint has altered sufficiently to affect its function, treatment may be aimed at alleviating the symptoms rather than curing the condition.

In the field of human medicine, success of such treatment may be measured by a degree of improvement that enables the patient to lead as near normal a life as possible. The sufferer from osteoarthritis seldom demands that he be restored to a state whereby he may enter the field of competitive sport. How different is the case of the racehorse! Treatment that merely enables a two- or three-year-old thoroughbred to walk in comfort is of little value when the animal's prime role is to run in races.

Treatment of early inflammation in a joint is exactly the same as treatment of inflammation in any other tissue, principally rest and cold applications. In the case of joints, it is extremely important to reduce the inflammation as rapidly as possible in order to protect the important structures within from further injury which might result in the condition becoming chronic. To this end, it is often an advantage to draw off some of the excess synovial fluid in order to relieve the pressure within the joint.

A relatively recent approach to the treatment of degenerative joint disease and injuries to joints is to inject hyaluronic acid or similar substances. This therapy is based on knowledge that the synovial fluid is composed of substances which act to lubricate as well as to nourish cartilage forming the joint surfaces. To counteract this, special substances which replace the natural protective substances can be introduced artificially by injection. This approach may be preceded by washing out the joint with a solution, such as normal saline, which removes the adverse substances. A similar means of protecting the joint surface and aiding the repair process is to inject special substances involved in the formation of cartilage. These substances, known as glycosaminoglycans may be injected intramuscularly and it is usual to give a course of six or seven injections at about four-day intervals.

In addition, the analysis of synovial fluid may give some indication of the degree of injury, and aid the veterinary surgeon in making a prognosis. Because it is not possible to put a horse to bed, complete rest is not practicable. The horse should remain in its box or be given light walking exercise. The time honoured method of applying 'cold' to a leg (namely the cold water hose), although still widely used, is now supplemented by the use of anti-inflammatory drugs. The commonest of these in veterinary use are the corticosteroids (cortisone) and butazolidin (bute). Treatment with these drugs often produces a dramatic improvement in the appearance of the joint, especially when cortisone is introduced directly into the joint space. Although cortisone injections may have a dramatic effect in relieving the pain, they cause damage to the joint surface so that their continued use may result in a very much worsened condition. For this reason, injections of cortisone into the joint are not usually recommended by veterinarians other than in exceptional circumstances. Although the signs of inflammation, heat and pain, are quickly removed by bute, time is essential for the proper healing of the injured tissues. Once the initial inflammation has been overcome, healing will be accelerated by heat treatment.

Early cases of degenerative joint disease due to injury of the joint capsule and minimal damage to the cartilage usually respond well to treatment as long as the animal is not returned to strenuous training too quickly. In the case of a valuable two-year-old with possible classic potential, it is often worth abandoning all attempts at serious training until the animal has gained a greater degree of maturity.

Unfortunately, in many cases, it is not until quite severe changes have already taken place in a joint that the horse becomes lame. These changes are irreversible and at present there is no treatment which can restore the joint to its normal state. The approach to cases of chronic arthritis depends mainly on the severity of the bony changes within the joint. If these are producing mechanical interference, either by virtue of their size and position, or due to the presence of small fractured fragments within the joint, conservative treatment is unlikely to be successful. Even surgical removal of the offending portions tends to give disappointing results. More often than not the animal, if suitable, is retired to stud.

Arthroscopy is a relatively new technique whereby special instruments are inserted in the joint under general anaesthesia. These comprise a straight tube through which the surgeon can see the content of the joint. A second tube is introduced at an angle and this may be used as a channel for fluid to wash out the joint and also as a means of placing an instrument into the joint to remove any fragments or scrape its surface surgically, depending on the requirements of the surgeon. Arthroscopy is a technique that may be used in place of cutting open the joint surgically, thereby achieving the desired effect through a relatively tiny incision.

Some horses, chronically unsound as a result of joint disease, can be kept in training with the judicious use of anti-inflammatory drugs. However, the use of such drugs to produce temporary artificial relief from lameness in order to allow a horse to race is open to criticism, from both veterinarians and the breeding industry. On the one hand, drugs are being used to mask disease processes by symptomatic treatment and, on the other, they may be enabling potential stud animals to win races under false colours.

It could be argued that horses in training, especially geldings, are useful for one purpose only - to run in races. In America, the problem of running horses under medication for degenerative joint disease has been a matter of concern for the racing boards of many states for some time. Many such bodies have now drawn up regulations and recommendations for the guidance of trainers and vets.

Prevention is better than any form of treatment and, where the condition is difficult or unsatisfactory to treat, this is especially true. However, to prevent a disease such as degenerative joint disease or at least to reduce its incidence, it is necessary to know considerably more about it than we do at the present time. It is known that the direct existing cause is the stress on the joints produced by training and racing, but behind that are several underlying or predisposing causes that result in one horse becoming arthritic while another remains sound. One of the most important is poor conformation, resulting in unequal pressure and wear on the joints. Such conformation is often inherited. We also know that certain nutritional deficiencies or imbalances can cause abnormalities of bones and joints. The importance of this has been accentuated by the 'forcing' of young stock in preparation for the sales. Possibly linked with the hereditary and nutritional aspects, is the degree of bone maturity of the yearling when it enters the racing stable. X-ray examination of the knees of large numbers of yearlings have shown that the degree of maturity varies considerably from individual to individual.

Perhaps part of the answer lies in the more drastic culling of bad-legged, arthritis-prone families from stud farms, a full investigation into the correct feeding of young thoroughbreds and a postponement of training in the cases of two-year-olds that show bone immaturity.

8: Treatment of limb fractures

Many people ask why, when a horse breaks a leg, it may have to be destroyed and why its limb cannot be mended in the same way as a human limb. The answer to the first question is the need to save unnecessary suffering, or because the injury will permanently prevent the horse from performing the work for which it is kept. The answer to the second is that in many cases we do mend limbs, even to the extent of being able to return the horse to the racecourse and see it remain sound for years after the injury. In only a small proportion of cases do we encounter a complete failure for treatment. They are the extreme cases which, understandably, tend to distress the general public.

There are more than 20 different bones in each leg of the horse and they vary greatly in size and shape, from those that are relatively long, such as the humerus and the radius, which between them form the elbow joint, to those that are short and small. Examples of these small bones are the two sesamoid bones at the back of the fetlock joint, and the carpal bones of the 'knee'. Any one or more of these bones may become broken or fractured as a result of injury and obviously the possibility of repair depends on which particular one is affected. In general, the larger the bone and the higher up in the limb, the more difficult it is to mend.

Another decisive factor is the nature or severity of the break. For example, the bone may fracture with a 'hairline' separation, and may be likened to a piece of china which is still serving a useful function, or it may be shattered into several widely separate pieces. In the most severe cases, the severed ends of the bone may come through the overlying skin, forming an open or compound fracture.

In deciding whether or not to treat a horse with a broken bone, the economic consequences have to be weighed. Will the horse be sound enough to race again, or to perform useful work such as hunting or hacking? If not, has it any value at stud as a stallion or brood mare and will the fracture heal sufficiently to prevent the animal being subject to chronic pain for the rest of its life? In many cases, only time, perhaps 6 months or a year, can provide the answer to these questions. In the meantime, the case must be treated immediately or a decision made to destroy the horse on humane grounds. Nowadays, owners are becoming more co-operative in allowing the veterinary surgeon to attempt treatment of the more severe types of fracture. Considerable improvement is thereby being achieved in the techniques of repair, as the profession learns by experience.

Other incentives behind the drive for improved results in fracture repair include the value of individuals for salvage for stud purposes. High values affect, for example, the attitude of the insurance market and underwriters are keen that every practical and humane means of salvaging injured subjects be practised. Specialist practices and centres at university veterinary schools are now increasingly equipped with the necessary facilities staffed by appropriate orthopaedic experts.

Whichever bone in the body is broken, the process of healing is the same. The ends become cemented together by the formation of new bone known as callus. The latter is formed first of soft tissue rather similar to scar tissue in which calcium is deposited, so eventually rendering it hard and 'bony'. Once formed, the callus unites the pieces of bone so that the resulting union makes the part as strong, if not stronger, than before.

A callus will take many weeks to harden, and it is essential that during this time the broken ends of the bones do not move, otherwise the repair will not be effective, or the result will be a crooked limb. The treatment of fractured bones is therefore aimed at immobilising the part so that there is no movement of the fractured ends on each other. There are several methods available to surgeons in the treatment of fractures. The best known is the plaster of paris cast, a soft bandage which is wrapped wet around the outside of the limb and which hardens on drying to form a firm support above and below the fracture.

Another method is to screw metal plates across the fractured ends of the bone underneath the skin, so fixing them together. Or, if it is a long bone, to place a steel pin down the centre marrow cavity to form an internal support. If a small piece of bone becomes detached from the main part, as for example may occur in the sesamoid bones, it is better to remove the chip surgically. Unless it is removed, the horse is unlikely to become completely sound.

During the last 20 years the technique of internal fixation has become increasingly used by veterinary orthopaedic surgeons. This technique consists of using screws, plates and pins, singly or in combination. The horse is anaesthetised and the fracture exposed by an incision through the skin. Depending on the nature and position of the fracture, a decision is made as to the exact means of fixation appropriate to the case. Any small chips or splinters of bone are usually removed during the procedure for fixation. If there are numerous splinters they may be left *in situ* although there is the risk that a detached spicule may become devitalised and cause a problem in healing.

Healing depends to a large extent on the ends of the bones being fixed so that they cannot move against each other. To be successful, the bone must heal in the original shape and with no abnormal angulation. Where the fracture has entered a joint, the union must restore the normal smooth contour of the joint surface. Internal fixation provides a more appropriate means to achieve such objectives than does splinting with a cast alone. Casts are often applied following internal fixation. Nowadays, the material used is much lighter and stronger than the old plaster of paris material.

These surgical methods have been made possible by improved anaesthetic techniques, allowing patients to be kept asleep for long periods, by the development of operating theatres free of dust, and by the use of antibiotics. Such methods are in common use in the hospitals, but horses, unlike human patients, present two major problems: (1) They do not co-operate by limiting freedom of movement, and (2) the forces involved when a horse contracts its muscles or puts its weight on a limb are relatively enormous. Any structure such as a plaster cast or metal plate which is used to obtain immobilisation of the part must be exceptionally strong.

As far as treatment is concerned, a combination of these two disadvantages may render a fracture case hopeless. A further problem of removal arises when a horse with a shattered bone has to be transported from a racecourse or wherever the injury has occurred. Modern tranquilising drugs and horse ambulances have made their contributions but there are always likely to be limitations as to what can be achieved.

9: Unsoundness

In 1967, when this book was first written, soundness was a term that had been employed for over 100 years as a basis on which horses were purchased or sold. However, with the enactment of trade description and misrepresentation legislation, it was argued that to certify a horse as 'sound' was to put oneself in the position of giving a guarantee on a par with certifying that a can contained a specified number of beans. If the purchaser found that the can contained a smaller number, the manufacturer and vendor of the can could be held liable in law for misrepresentation.

Obviously this interpretation of the law put veterinary surgeons into considerable difficulty. It was therefore agreed within the profession, in consultation with lawyers and insurers against professional liabilities, that the term 'suitable for purchase' should replace 'soundness'. Further, the Royal College of Veterinary Surgeons (RCVS) advised members that they should not provide certificates of examination which would be available for prospective purchasers at auctions. The reason given was that there should be a direct relationship between the prospective purchaser and the veterinarian involved in the examination.

This did not prevent an owner giving a warranty of health and fitness or of suitability for a particular performance or function which could be used by a new owner if the terms of the warranty did not appear to have been met.

The modern approach to the previous 'soundness examinations' at time of sale is to follow the procedure of examination recommended by the Royal College of Veterinary Surgeons/British Veterinary Association. Forms are available for completion at the end of the examination and all defects, abnormalities or unusual findings must be recorded. This still leaves the vet free to give an opinion based on the interpretation of his findings in the examination.

Whatever phraseology is used in the course of these interpretations it is the vet's conclusions upon which the decision regarding a sale is based. The term 'soundness' may have gone out of fashion but it remains the principle upon which the examinations take place, even today. Horses are still 'vetted' and the time-honoured term belongs to the veterinary surgeon.

Because this spirit remains intact, and is likely to do so for many years to come, the following account written in 1966 is still relevant and is therefore reproduced for the reader's interest, with comments in italics indicating changes in present practice:

Wherever you go in the world of horsemen, the expressions 'sound' or 'soundness' are frequently heard. 'Sound in all respects', 'sound in eyes, wind and limb', 'sold subject to being passed sound by the vet', are phrases familiar to horsemen the world over. At public sales, the auctioneer would once announce that 'this horse is warranted sound' or that 'there is a soundness certificate lodged in the office, signed by Mr So and So, Veterinary Surgeon'.

A vet cannot now certify horses for auction as explained above.

What is this term that is used so frequently and upon which so much importance is placed? Soundness is concerned with health and disease, the normal and the abnormal. It is intimately connected with those very problems which are the main points of discussion in this book. In particular, soundness is related to whether or not an individual has a defect which will interfere with the function or usefulness for which that animal is used. For instance, does the lump which can be felt on the cannon bone or at the back of a hock mean that the animal will not be able to race successfully? Does the noise we hear when the horse breathes indicate that there will be interference with the performance of that animal when it is subjected to racing conditions?

Alternatively, in a non-racing animal, will a defect interfere with its performance in the show ring or the hunting field? If the answer to the question is that the defect will, in fact, impair performance, we say that the horse is unsound. If, on the other hand, there is no defect present which will cause such a loss of performance, the horse is said to be sound.

It might seem to the reader that the problem is a matter of knowing the purpose to which any particular individual is to be put, and whether there is a defect or disease present which will reduce the capacity of the horse to carry out that purpose. But in practice, this simplified approach to soundness is as unworkable as King Canute's idea for restraining the tides! If we consider the reasons why this is so, it will give us some idea of the complex nature of the problems involved.

Everyone connected with horses is, in one way or another, interested in whether or not a horse is sound - the breeder, the agent, the lad who looks after the horse, the bookmaker, the betting public, even the stewards may all have an interest in whether or not a particular individual can give his maximum performance or if this is impaired by unsoundness. The pockets of the buyer and seller are touched to a material extent, and when controversy arises, it is the buyer and seller (and sometimes an agent or an auctioneer) who become involved.

The disputes that have been fought in the courts and in which rulings have been given by judges has led to certain legal definitions for the terms 'soundness' or 'unsoundness'. For example, in the 'Hamama' Case, Mr Justice Paull quoted from an earlier judgement of Baron Parke: 'I have always considered that a man buying a horse warranted sound must be taken as buying him for immediate use, and he has a right to expect one capable of that use and of being immediately put to any fair work the owner chooses. The rule as to unsoundness is that, if at the time of the sale, the horse has any disease which either actually does diminish the natural usefulness of the animal, so as to make him less capable of work of any description, or which in its ordinary progress will diminish the natural usefulness of the animal, or if the horse has, either from disease or accident, undergone any alteration of structure that either actually does at the time, or in its ordinary effects will diminish the natural usefulness of the horse, such a horse is unsound'.

In addition, Mr Paull quoted Baron Alderson: 'The word "sound" means sound, and the only qualification of which it is susceptible arises from the purpose for which the warranty is given. If, for instance, a horse is purchased to be used in a given way, the word sound means that the animal is useful for that purpose, and unsound means that he is at the time affected with something which will have the effect of impeding that use'.

Mr Justice Paull, in his summing up, commented on unsoundness as applied to a particular organ of the body, such as the heart: 'You do not warrant that a horse has a heart which will remain sound during the horse's life, or that the heart is so strongly built that it is unlikely to break down at some future date. You warrant that at the moment of sale the heart is not then diseased and that the heart is fit for work of the kind to which the vendor has reason to believe the horse may reasonably be put in the immediate future'.

In every transaction where a horse changes ownership it is natural for the purchaser at least to require some guarantee that the article for which he is paying is genuine. Just as the prospective purchaser of a house or a car requires some form of guarantee that there are no structural defects, so the purchaser of a horse expects to have some form of protection. Unfortunately where living animals are concerned it is quite impossible to arrive at a comparable degree of protection or guarantee. Protection by soundness examinations is tending to fall further and further into disrepute. One firm of bloodstock auctioneers will not even sell a horse under such a guarantee and it relies entirely on the principle of 'let the buyer beware'. *Many auctioneers make it a condition of sale that a horse can be returned if it makes an abnormal respiratory sound characteristic of whistling or roaring.*

Auctioneers certainly cannot be blamed for taking the attitude that they do not wish to become involved in lengthy and unpleasant disputes. But, on the other hand, persons who are prepared to pay large sums of money for horses are entitled to as great a degree of protection against intended or unintended fraud as the ingenuity of man can devise.

The sale of fake Renoirs or Rembrandts would bring no credit to anyone concerned and, in the long run, would weaken confidence within the trade. But if the desire on the part of the horse-owning public to have some system of guarantee is justified and reasonable, it is all the more important that they should co-operate with the veterinary profession in establishing one that is likely to succeed. It is, after all, the veterinary surgeon whose task it is to examine the horse and pronounce whether or not he is sound.

What, in fact, are the problems that face the veterinary surgeon? The first question that a vet has to ask himself when examining animals for soundness is the purpose for which the animal is being examined. In other words, is he certifying it sound for racing, for breeding, or for some other purpose such as for hacking, the show ring or hunting field? On this knowledge, he will base the type of examination to which he will subject the horse in order to give his opinion. For instance, in order to pass an opinion as to whether a horse is sound for stud purposes, it is necesary, in addition to being satisfied as to his general health, to know whether his libido, or sexual drive, is normal, that he can mount and serve a mare, and that the quality of his semen is such that he is likely to be fertile. For an animal not required for racing, it is not necessary to subject him to severe exercise tests. In the end, a vet's conclusions are essentially a matter of opinion. But the greater the amount of known facts on which the opinion is based, the more likely is the opinion to be correct.

The opinion is thus a conclusion based on the evidence obtained from the examination and, although held with confidence, it must necessarily always fall short of absolute knowledge or certainty.

In collecting evidence on which to base his opinion, the vet is only too well aware of both the frailties and adaptability of living tissue. A structure which is apparently normal at the time of examination may succumb to stresses imposed on it the very next time that the horse is worked or, alternatively, an observed defect in any part may quite unexpectedly withstand the same pressures for years because other structures compensate for the weakness.

How does the present system work and is it sufficient for modern needs? The answer most responsible people would give is no!

As progress is made and scientific discoveries are increasingly applied to veterinary medicine, so the problem of how far the veterinary surgeon should go in collecting evidence for soundness examinations before giving an opinion is a matter of urgent concern. It should be clear that it is often necessary to go beyond the scope of our clinical senses (ie eyes, ears and touch) in order to ascertain the exact nature of the ailment. For instance, in order to diagnose accurately an enlargement in the knee or in the so-called splint region it may be necessary to make an X-ray examination or confirm or differentiate between one condition and another, it is often necessary to resort to specialised examinations and to laboratory techniques.

One of the difficulties that must be faced is the cost of the examination. This is bound to increase with the length and intensity of the examination. It is recognised that, while cost may not be a limitation in the case of valuable racehorses, the same cannot be said to apply in the case of a child's pony.

Although reappraisal of the system is obviously necessary, there is one area in which the lay public tends to place a stultifying hand on the profession - its attitude towards the vet both with regard to the examination and in the conclusions that he may make as a result. Every man may, on occasions, think himself to be an authority on soundness. During the 19th century an experienced horseman was on equal terms with the vet. Both could use the experience of their eyes, ears and hands to discover and assess the evidence from which to make an opinion. Many lay persons today are loathe to give up this equality, refusing to admit the part now played by scientific methods. It is a common experience for the vet to be told before he even enters the horse's box that, 'this horse is sound' or 'his heart is quite all right' and so on. Statements may come from the lad, the trainer, or the owner and are not always a gambit to intimidate, but a genuine feeling that they are in a better position, or at least one just as good, to judge as the veterinary surgeon. Probably as a result of this attitude, some owners place limitations on what they consider should or should not be done during the soundness examination. Woe betide the veterinary surgeon who does more or less than is considered traditionally correct.

Similarly, there is often a traditionally-held belief as to what should or should not be written on the soundness certificate and what is to be considered an unsoundness. Many people like to have every abnormality or defect that the veterinary surgeon may find exhibited on the certificate. To state the findings that differ from the normal state, such as curbs, splints etc, when the examination is confined to a visual inspection is one thing but, if we are to advance into the modern age, the examinations will become increasingly more searching and the evidence obtained more technical. For example, in the examination of the heart, increasing knowledge concerning the differentiation of the significance of one heart murmur from another would lead to confusion if the lay public continued to demand the publication of all the evidence on which the opinion of soundness was based. Often, the mere mention of the presence of a murmur is enough to condemn an animal in some people's minds.

What is the answer? Should there be a system where varying shades or degrees of soundness are recognised? How much information with regard to the defects that are found during the soundness examination does the public require to know? In many cases the veterinary surgeon may be required to submit a certificate stating that the horse is either sound or unsound without ever being consulted by the purchaser. In fact, everything must be in black and white with no shades of grey allowed. As, in these circumstances, the vet cannot discuss his findings with the man who is actually buying the horse, any abnormality becomes a possible source of grievance for the new owner when the horse arrives in his new home. 'I won't have a horse with splints, but I don't mind curbs' may be the categorical attitude of one owner, but the reverse may be the case with another. *It is this difficulty which has now been resolved by prohibiting vets from issuing certificates under circumstances of sale by auction as discussed above.*

Without direct communication, it is difficult to get an examination and certificate worded to suit everybody! To state some of the problems is not, of course, to solve them, but their solution can only come through the knowledge of their existence and a better understanding of their basic causes.

Whatever method the intending horse buyer sees fit to employ in order to protect himself from buying 'a pig in a poke', the previous history of the animal is of immense importance. This applies whether he makes his own examination or relies on professional advice. If the reader were to go to his own doctor and ask for a 'soundness examination' for insurance purposes, detailed knowledge of previous medical history would be required. The validity of soundness in horses would be immeasurably increased if some background information was likewise provided before the veterinary surgeon was expected to put his name to a certificate. Under present conditions he is, by tradition, expected to give an opinion based on an examination lasting perhaps an hour, and having no previous knowledge of the animal whatsoever.

If the animal suffers from bouts of colic, recurrent lameness, or breaks blood vessels there is certainly no obligation on the part of the vendor to reveal these facts, although it is quite probable that there will be no evidence detected during a physical examination at any particular time. Continuing the analogy of the doctor, epilepsy, migraine, or grumbling appendix are unlikely to be suspected without some medical history, or unless the patient is actually suffering an attack at the time of examination.

At the present time, the horse-owning community appears to be governed by rather incomprehensible moral attitudes concerning the information that vendors should give at public auctions. It is, for instance, apparently considered proper for the vendor to state that the horse has had a hobday operation before it is sold. On the other hand, it is not necessary to state that it makes a respiratory noise or whistle. *It is now necessary for vendors to make a statement regarding horse's wind at auction otherwise the horse may be returned by the purchaser.* The paradox in this moral distinction is that while it is possible to feel the scar in an animal which has been hobdayed, it is impossible to detect a wind infirmity unless the horse is heard whilst it is galloping. An impartial observer might be forgiven for thinking that bloodstock sales were conducted in circumstances in which the detection of a defective animal is made as difficult as is consistent with not appearing to be downright immoral in the process! Under these circumstances a yearling can be sold for thousands of pounds with a fracture of one of its sesamoid bones, on the grounds that the seller may be ignorant of the fact or that the buyer is entitled to view the animal prior to the sale. 'Let the buyer beware' is one thing, but at least the purchaser must be allowed the best and most proper circumstances of investigation.

Some people even seem to regard the inspection of their horses prior to sale as a privilege which they extend to a prospective purchaser provided he behaves himself according to their own rules! The deeper the investigation, the more tiresome it will be for such sellers. There are, however, a number of simple examinations which could be made professionally in order to facilitate the protection of purchasers. For instance, a filly out of training need only be examined once and the size of her ovaries stated, to ease the mind of a prospective purchaser that she has, in fact, got a pair capable of functioning and not so immature as to be of doubtful use. In yearlings and foals, a whole range of tests would be useful in assessing health status, including the radiology of any lumps, especially those around the knees and fetlocks. Various laboratory examinations could be used to demonstrate conclusively the health of the animal and freedom from such conditions as anaemia, which might be the result of a red worm infection. The presentation of such evidence would certainly be helpful to the prospective purchaser in deciding whether or not he should go to four or five figures for an animal.

While these particular investigations would necessarily have to be interpreted by vets, it is, nowadays, customary for the professional man to be asked for his opinion before a sale, so to make available information on this scale would therefore merely put him in a position to carry out his function in a more satisfactory and proper manner. In Australia, the use of the electrocardiogram for pre-sale examinations is a very good example of the introduction of the techniques of modern science in an attempt to establish means of differentiating between the good and bad, the healthy and unhealthy.

All these specialised techniques fail, however, if they are singled out to give an answer on their own to whether or not a horse should be bought. They can only be used to widen knowledge of the facts. The purchaser, with his professional adviser, can still be free to decide whether or not to ignore any one of them.

The use of radiography or other searching diagnostic technique before a sale is usually shunned by vendors because, as they argue, it might 'erroneously injure the sale' of one of their good animals, or because the methods advocated are 'impractical'. *Nowadays, under American influence, radiographs are frequently insisted upon in the sale of a racehorse and the seller usually agrees to having this examination performed.*

Unfortunately, the system as it stands today makes it difficult for a seller to put what he knows to be a genuine animal on the market and obtain a fair price, since it is known to everyone that quite a high proportion of animals that are auctioned are there because they have some very good reason for being culled. It would, therefore, be in the interest of sellers to improve the system whereby protection is given to buyers. After all, in the passing of defective animals, someone must take the rap at some stage, and although the wealthy owner may be able to afford the consequences of purchasing the occasional dud, the small owner may be risking his all.

The suggestion that the previous history of an animal should be made available, supported by the signature of both owner and vet, would, in fact, merely be an extension of the limited lines of investigation which are already in use. For instance, where horses in training are concerned, knowledge obtained from the form book is always used in an attempt to assess the previous history of the horse. Absence from a racecourse for a long period causes suspicion and demands an explanation. In such circumstances, even more careful note is taken of the limbs and especially swellings on the tendons or the joints, as indications of some unsoundness. A written statement by the owner to the effect that the horse had not been lame during the previous six months would help to sell a genuine article in these circumstances.

Similarly, the purchaser of a brood mare, while noting the general health of the animal and whether she has two eyes, a normal udder, no parrot jaw, good feet, well

Unsoundness

conformed vulva and no evidence of matted discharge on the tail or buttocks, also does well to look at the breeding history as recorded in the stud book. Here, information is recorded as to the years in which the mare has been barren, or had twins or dead foals. The prospective purchaser might further ask the seller of a 'mare-in-foal' to produce a certificate from his vet stating that at no time during the covering season was there evidence of streptococcal or other infections present in the mare's uterus.

10: Thoroughbred reproduction

It is well known that it is less easy to get mares to conceive in February, March and early April than in May, June, July and August. One of the principle reasons for this is the fact that during the first part of the year the ovaries are less active and tend not to produce eggs as they do in the warm spring and summer months.

To understand how and why the oestrous cycle occurs the reader must know something of the breeding organs and glands in the mare. The sexual organs of the mare consist of two ovaries which produce eggs and the uterus into which the spermatozoa are deposited by the stallion (Fig 10.1). The uterus is connected with each ovary by a fallopian tube, in one of which the egg is fertilised and down which it passes into the uterus. The latter also communicates with the exterior through the cervix and vagina. The function of the female sex organs is, therefore, the production of an egg, the acceptance of the male seed, the fertilisation of the egg and its development into a new individual.

When the ovaries become active, numerous fluid sacs (follicles) develop at the surface. Each of these contains an egg (ovum). Usually only one and, at most, two of these are large enough to become mature. The mature follicle ruptures at a specific point (ovulation fossa) in the ovary. The egg it contains is flushed into the fallopian tubes which have a funnel shaped opening. The egg is fertilised in the tube under suitable conditions if sperms are present. The fertilised egg then takes about 5 days to travel down the tube into the uterus.

The remaining follicles in the ovary do not rupture (ovulate) but gradually become smaller as their fluid is absorbed. The ovaries contain many thousand eggs at birth and most of these are lost over the course of the mare's natural life, either by being shed at each ovulation or because the follicles that contain them do not complete their development to maturity.

At the time of ovulation the egg is shed and passes down one of the two fallopian tubes into the uterus. If the egg is not fertilised by the sex cell of the stallion (spermatazoon), it will quickly die. As the egg is usually shed about 24h before the mare goes 'out of season' (by definition, a time when the mare will not accept the stallion, usually lasting 17 days), she must be mated before the egg is shed. The spermatozoa of the stallion live in the mare's uterus for only a limited time, which depends partly on the 'quality' of the stallion's semen and partly on the state of the mare's uterus.

The quality of semen depends upon its volume and the number of live normal motile sperm it contains. Upon these measures depend the fertilising capacity of each ejaculation of semen. Some stallions have semen of lower quality than others. This is often reflected in their capacity to obtain conception in harem mares. High quality denotes semen which contains large numbers of sperm which can live and remain active for several days whereas in poor quality the sperm live for only hours rather than days. Infection or adverse secretions in the mare's uterus shorten the length of life of the spermatozoa. Their length of life varies from perhaps a few hours to as long as seven days but for practical purposes it is usual to expect some at least to live for about two or three days. However, as the egg dies within 24h of being shed and the sperm has to meet the egg in the fallopian tube to fertilise it, it is best for the mating to take place within a day, or possibly two, before ovulation occurs.

During the early part of the stud season the duration of oestrus may be many days. Thus there is a good opportunity for a mating to occur several days before ovulation. In this case the sperm may die before having the opportunity to fertilise the egg. In the spring and summer months the duration is usually shortest, varying from three to five days. However, individuals vary and some have a period of a day, others of eight days or more. Because timing of mating is essential to provide the optimum chance of conception, veterinary examinations are helpful.

These examinations consist of rectal palpation. The vet inserts a gloved and lubricated arm into the rectum of the mare and can readily feel the ovaries. The follicles may be felt and their size determined by this method. It is therefore possible by repeated examination to follow the maturity of the follicle throughout the oestrous period, thereby enabling the veterinarian to provide advice as to the best time for mating. It is also possible to determine that ovulation has occurred and therefore that the mare is coming to the end of her oestrous period, which usually follows 24-48h afterwards.

Such examinations often show that no follicle is present in the ovary although the mare may well be in oestrous. If there is no follicle and consequently no possibility of an egg being shed, mating is not worth while and in this way it is possible to reduce wasteful services by stallions.

The control of the sexual cycle is by chemical substances known as hormones. These are substances produced by glands and which circulate in the blood stream and act on target organs. There are many different types of hormones produced by the glands and these are closely involved in a wide range of living functions. A well-known example is insulin, which is produced by special cells in the pancreas and which is concerned with the level of sugar in the bloodstream.

The hormones responsible for the sexual behaviour of the mare include oestrogen and progesterone, both of which are produced from different parts of the

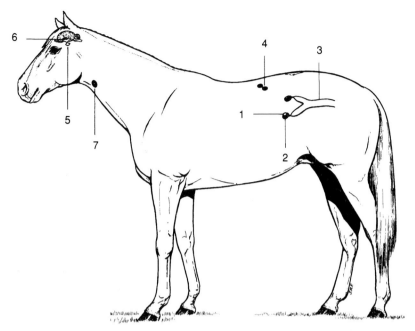

Fig 10.1: Reproduction in the mare (1) ovarian follicle, (2) yellow body,
(3) prostaglandin from the lining of the uterus, (4) adrenal glands, (5) pituitary gland,
(6) hypothalamus, and (7) thyroid gland

ovaries. In addition, the pituitary gland produces two hormones, follicle stimulating hormone (FSH) and luteinising hormone (LH). FSH acts on the ovary, promoting the growth of a follicle which contains the egg, due to be shed under the influence of LH which influences the follicle to rupture. Other hormones, known as gonadotrophin-releasing hormones (GnRH) are produced by special cells in the brain within the region known as the hypothalamus. GnRH hormone causes the pituitary gland to release FSH and LH.

During the time that the follicle is ripening under the action of FSH the ovary is producing oestrogen, which is responsible for the signs of oestrous, including the lubrication of the genital tract in preparation for acceptance of the male organ. After ovulation has occurred, under the influence of LH, the uterus is prepared for pregnancy by the action of the hormone progesterone, secreted by the lining of the ruptured follicle (yellow body or corpus luteum). This hormone is responsible for the maintenance of pregnancy. After about the 120th day from conception, it is also produced by the placenta in sufficient quantities to maintain pregnancy without the assistance of the ovaries.

In the absence of conception (fertilisation of the egg) the lining of the uterus produces a hormone known as prostaglandin. This travels to the ovary where it causes the yellow body to dissolve. As the yellow body ceases to produce progesterone the next oestrous cycle starts and the mare comes into heat. The sexual behaviour of the mare (the signs which tell us whether the mare is in season or not in season) reflect the hormonal control and alternating influence of oestrogen and progesterone.

It seems that the pituitary gland plays the dominating role in the control of the hormonal system as far the sex organs are concerned. It has been likened to the conductor of the orchestra and it is thought to be the gland which mediates between internal events within the mare and the outside world. For instance, length of daylight, temperature and other climatic conditions in the environment play a direct part in the stimulation of the pituitary gland and the production of FSH. The concentration of the various hormones within the bloodstream at a given point dictates the predominant character of the mare's sexual behaviour at that time. The very predominance of each hormone will, however, stimulate the gland to produce the opposing factors, so that a cycle of behaviour is produced which we call the sexual cycle.

During oestrous, the follicle is developing under the influence of FSH and oestrogen hormone is in the ascendancy. At the end of that time, which lasts some five days, ovulation is caused by the influence of LH. Soon afterwards, the mare goes into a state of dioestrous, or being out of season, during which time she will not accept the male. This latter behaviour is largely the result of progesterone. The time of being out of season lasts for 17 days and the whole cycle recurs unless the egg has been fertilised. In this case, oestrous is not usually seen again until pregnancy has terminated.

We know that there are only very small levels of hormones in the blood, which yet produce profound changes in the body. The exact levels which produce an effect are unknown. In any case, they vary from individual to individual, because the action of a particular hormone depends as much upon the sensitivity of the target organ as upon the amount of hormone reaching the target. For example, the response of the mare's genital organs to oestrogens circulating in her bloodstream is very much influenced by the number of receptor sites by which the oestrogen can attach to the membranes and muscles of the organ. Oestrogen may be likened to keys and the receptors to locks. The action of the key depends on it finding a lock into which it will fit.

Progesterone and oestrogen belong to a chemical order of hormones known as steroids. There are about 30 known hormones in this group, including the male sex hormone, and the capacity of the body to interchange these substances under different conditions is well known. In fact, the male sex hormone has been found in quite high concentration in the fluid of the mare's follicle. A disorder of the sexual cycle and behaviour pattern of the mare with regard to mating may therefore be symptoms of a derangement of the complex hormonal control.

Dealing with a problem arising from a hormonal imbalance is far from straightforward. Balance cannot be restored merely by supplying in artificial form one or other of the sex hormones. However, hormone therapy has advanced during the last decade and we are now able to manipulate the sexual behaviour of mares in a way which was hardly possible 20 or 30 years ago. Synthetic progesterone with a very powerful action may be used to stimulate the start of oestrous periods in a mare that is undergoing a quiescent or winter phase. Similarly, synthetic GnRH hormones may be used to trigger the development of follicles in the ovary, while luteinising hormone can artificially shorten an oestrous period by causing the mare to ovulate if a suitable follicle is present in the ovary at the time the injection is made.

In treatment of mares, we must distinguish between those therapies aimed at manipulating the oestrous cycle and those required to treat infertility. These aspects are considered in succeeding chapters.

11: Natural breeding season

It is natural for most species of animals to have a breeding season. In the horse, this is during the late spring and early summer months. The foal is thus born when grass is plentiful and the weather kind to a newborn. The start of the thoroughbred stud season in this country is 15 February. From that date until 15 July mares are mated with the stallion at thoroughbred studs throughout the British Isles and, indeed, in most countries in the northern hemisphere. There are two basic reasons why 15 February has been chosen, the first being an artificial one. The rules of the Stud Book kept by Weatherby's and the Rules of Racing dictate that the birthday of all thoroughbreds be 1 January. On that day an animal becomes a year older. Therefore, a foal born on 31 December would, officially, become a yearling on the following day.

The second reason is a natural one, arising from the fact that the average length of pregnancy (gestation) in the mare is 11 months. However, it is not uncommon for a foal to be born 15 days prior to this average. There is a strong possibility, therefore, that a mare mated before 15 February will produce a foal before 1 January. Such a foal would be at a disadvantage for many years, being forced to compete in races alongside horses a year older.

During the natural mating season, mares will accept the male for about five days, at intervals of 2.5-3 weeks. The period of acceptance is known as oestrus, 'heat' or 'being in season' and the interval between is known as dioestrus, or 'being out of heat or season'. This alternating pattern is known as the oestrous, or sexual cycle, and it normally continues throughout the months of the mating season unless conception occurs. Once the mare becomes pregnant, the cycle ceases. Thereafter, the mare does not normally show signs of oestrus until about nine days after foaling. This first heat after foaling is often referred to as the foaling heat.

Outside the months of the mating season, from late summer to early spring, the natural tendency for mares is to be anoestrus, that is to say not to show signs of being in season. Individuals may show marked variations, so that oestrus may occur at any time during the year, in cycles of abnormal length and irregularity.

In the wild state, the stallion runs with his mares, mating with them at times of his own choosing, dictated by the instincts which tell him that the mare is in the receptive state of oestrus. On thoroughbred stud farms in this and most other countries, the stallion is kept apart from his mares and the mating programme is therefore entirely man-controlled. The time of mating is artificially selected so that any departure from normal behaviour will be more likely in itself to lead to barrenness.

Trying or teasing are the names given to the process whereby the mare is brought into the presence of a male horse (known as a teaser) in order to stimulate her into showing whether or not she is in oestrus. This ritual is carried out each or every other day on all the main thoroughbred studs during the breeding season of February to July. It falls to the lot of the stud groom to study the sexual behaviour of the mares under his control and to decide whether or not they are showing signs of oestrus. In most cases he can, nowadays, call on the help of the veterinary surgeon and the fact that such assistance is so often necessary illustrates the difficulties which are encountered.

The mare is essentially an animal with herd instincts. Alternating periods of solitary confinement and being turned into unknown paddocks with 'strangers' for company at haphazard intervals, depending on the necessary whims of stud management, may interfere with the normal regular pattern of behaviour. Because mares and stallions are kept separately to avoid any possible risk of injury to a valuable stallion which might occur if an attempted mating took place while the mare was not in oestrus, a system has necessarily had to be devised whereby the stud groom must satisfy himself as to the stage each individual has reached in her sexual cycle. The routine of trying mares for perhaps a minute or two each day and by a horse which will not, in fact, be the one which is used for mating, seems to be a process which is resented by some mares.

When the mare becomes pregnant, the sexual cycle is suppressed and she does not again show in season until nine days after producing the foal she has conceived. The process of trying or teasing is intended as an indicator to help decide which point of the mare's cycle has been reached at any particular time. The mare is placed on one side of a solid gate or panel in a fence and introduced to the teaser which stands on the other side. The teaser is usually an entire horse and may be a thoroughbred of little value, or a pony or arab stallion kept specially for the purpose. In this way, continual contact of the valuable thoroughbred stallion with his mares is avoided, every effort being taken to prevent a mare who is not in a receptive state being presented to him in the stallion yard thus risking injury.

The mare's sexual status will be indicated by a distinct show of repugnance or

Natural breeding season

Fig 11.1: When not in 'use', the mare will show signs of violence towards the teaser

Fig 11.2: Characteristics shown when the mare is in 'use'

Natural breeding season

47

acceptance when the teaser displays his natural pre-mating attitudes towards her - biting and nuzzling against her flanks, and whinnying and sniffing round her quarters. Some breeders permit the teaser to 'talk' to the mare; that is, to place the two head-on over the bar, in the position that horses approach each other in the natural state. When a mare is not in 'use' she will resent the teaser, laying her ears back, swishing her tail, baring her teeth and kicking violently, which is, of course, the reason for the barrier between them (Fig 11.1). When a mare is in 'use' she will indicate her state by leaning towards the teaser, standing straddle-legged in the breeding position, and lengthening the vulva, from which mucus may appear (Fig 11.2).

If mares were machinery there might be a clockwork precision about the sexual cycle and the process of teasing would merely be a matter of presenting the mare to the teaser and obtaining a certain response, according to the time of the cycle. Living creatures do not, however, behave like automated time switches. In practice there is a wide variety in the degree of readiness to 'show' to the teaser. So variable that it has truly been said that the only consistent fact about the breeding periods of mares is their inconsistency! Such inconsistency is exaggerated in thoroughbreds by man's contrariness in selecting a mating season which is quite unnatural for those being mated.

At the trying board, it is only to be expected, therefore, to see a wide range of behaviour, from mares 'drunk' at the barrier with long periods of oestrus lasting for days (possibly weeks), others not showing at all (although still ready to accept the stallion if taken to the covering), to those mares that are 'in' for a very short time, perhaps only for 12h or so.

Many of the difficulties encountered at the trying board are due to the very artificial way in which the mares are kept. For instance, some mares are very foal-proud and, when taken to the teaser, are much too anxious about their offspring left behind in the box to display their sexual feelings at the trying board. Others may stand at the teasing bar without showing particular interest either way, and in these cases it is probably only after several minutes that the rigorous attentions of the teaser will draw even the faintest reaction or indication that the mare is in oestrus. Another state of 'anxiety' which may cover up the normal display of feeling when mares are tried is the eagerness to get into the paddocks after being stabled all night. Some mares, possibly from habit, seem to sense that the teaser is a sham, and they will never show at the trying board, but only when taken into the covering yard and presented to the horse that is actually going to cover them.

Therefore, there are many mares which, by their absence of feeling at the board, fail to show that they are in season, whereas in fact they are.

Whilst most mares may give a genuine show, there is still quite a large minority over which considerable time and trouble must be spent before they will show properly, and it is true to say that of the three steps involved in breeding - teasing, foaling and covering - the most important is teasing. Without accurate and

Natural breeding season

painstaking attention to this particular operation, there can be no covering and, therefore, no foaling. Careful breeders will check their mare's sexual behaviour by teasing her every other day during the breeding season, regardless of whether she has been covered or is believed to be pregnant.

It is only by carrying out this routine that mares which have been cheating at the bar or who have cycles differing from the normal (5 days in, 17 days out) can be spotted, and measures taken to ensure that mating with the stallion takes place before the end of the season arrives.

During warmer weather and longer days, when the heat periods are likely to be shorter, it is a wise precaution to tease doubtful mares every day and even in some cases twice daily if time allows. In addition, careful observation of the mares while they are grazing in the paddocks will often give an indication as to their sexual states, as sometimes they will show to each other, even though they have behaved fiercely to the teaser.

Many mares are creatures of habit, and they will even show to the stud manager or stud groom, possibly associating him with the visits to the covering yard! A daily entry in a notebook of the results seen at the trying board is essential, and these records should also be transferred to a wall chart in the office. This will be a quick visual aid to the general teasing and covering position of all the mares on the stud.

12: Stud manager and vet

The examination of mares by veterinary surgeons during the breeding season has a number of objectives falling roughly into two categories: those aimed at giving advice to the manager and stud groom in the various decisions that they have to make in the day-to-day routine (such as the best time of mating a particular mare) and those of a veterinary or medical nature which involve the diagnosis and treatment of mares which have disease and abnormalities of their breeding organs (Fig 12.1 and 12.2). A close liaison has developed between vets and managements, resulting in a system of examinations carried out with varying degrees of intensity depending on the locality of the stud. Those in the large breeding centres tend to place a greater reliance and dependence on such a partnership than is perhaps the case in more isolated regions.

The examination of mares includes the following features:

(1) The palpation, or feeling, of the ovaries in order to find out whether or not there are ripe follicles present in the ovaries, or if ovulation has recently occurred.

(2) With the aid of an instrument known as a speculum making a visual examination of the vagina and cervix and confirming the exact point in the oestrus cycle, suggested by the mare's behaviour at the trying board. When a mare is in oestrus the cervix will be moist, reddened and relaxed, and the lining of the vagina lubricated with a small amount of slimy mucus. In contrast, when a mare is out of

Fig 12.1: Rectal examination of a mare. The uterus and ovaries can be felt by the veterinary surgeon with complete safety

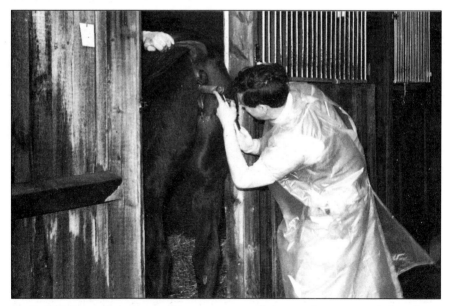

Fig 12.2: Vaginal examination. An instrument called a speculum is inserted, through which it is possible to see the vagina and cervix

Stud manager and vet

season the cervix will be contracted and pale, the lining of the vagina sticky.

(3) Supply additional evidence by the feel of the uterus, the walls of which are slack and thin when under the influence of the oestrus-producing hormone oestrogen, thick and turgid under the influence of progesterone, between the oestrus periods or when the mare is pregnant. In the latter case, a foetal sac can be felt as a soft swelling within one of the two horns of the uterus, increasing in size from about 17 days of pregnancy onwards.

(4) Besides a visual examination of the cervix, collecting material on a swab for examination under the microscope and culture in the laboratory. In this way, the presence and nature of any infection can be determined in what is normally a sterile part of the genital tract.

In practice, the information obtained from such examinations is used for a number of different purposes. These include the avoidance of unnecessary service in those cases that have no chance of conception, and enabling the stud manager to decide when each mare should be covered to give the best chance of conception. Selection of time is governed on the one hand by the fact that the sperm will die within two or three days of being deposited in the uterus and on the other, by the fact that the egg will die within 24 hours of being shed. In addition, where more than one follicle in the ovary is ripe at the same time, the stud manager may avoid the likely outcome of twins by refraining from having the mare covered during that particular oestrus. The mare's behaviour at the trying board can also be verified as genuine or not.

Perhaps the most important function of the examination is the early diagnosis of an infected mare, so avoiding the risk of infecting other mares or even the stallion. Also timely treatment of the individual can be carried out to avoid temporary or permanent infertility. During such examinations, the knowledge gained of what is happening in the ovaries, uterus and genital tract is also invaluable in arriving at a diagnosis for all forms of infertility and for their treatment.

How are the veterinary examinations performed? Most mares, especially if they are in season, do not resent the process and can be examined inside a loose box with only a bridle to restrain them. One man stands at the head and another holds the tail. A few mares show displeasure by directing at the examiner a painful kick. To give some protection, it is therefore usually the custom for the operator to examine mares either in stocks or round a doorpost. In rare cases, it may be necessary to apply other forms of restraint such as a 'twitch'.

In order to feel the ovaries and the uterus, the veterinary surgeon, wearing a long-sleeved rubber glove well lubricated with soap, inserts his arm into the rectum and removes any dung which is present. It is then quite easy to feel the genital organs through the wall of the rectum. The vagina and cervix are examined with the use of a speculum after the superficial areas have been well cleaned with disinfectant. As the insertion of the speculum breaks down the valve-like arrangement formed by the vulva and the pelvis which normally prevents air from being taken into the vagina,

it is essential to examine mares in an atmosphere free of dust and contamination. When examining a mare 'in oestrus', a sterile swab in a protective case can easily be passed in the cervix and a bacteriological examination made.

The vet takes detailed notes of his findings at the time of the examination: the size of the ovaries, the presence of follicles, together with their approximate diameter and whether they feel tense or soft. He will also note the position of the follicles within the ovary for, in general, the closer they lie to the ovulation fossa, the sooner they can be expected to ovulate, whatever their size. Descriptions of the state of the vagina, cervix, uterus, vulva, etc, are also made so that, with the help of the notes taken over whole series of examinations during different times of the oestrus cycle, an accurate diagnosis can be made of any trouble or abnormality in the genital organs. Most veterinary surgeons use abbreviations in order to save time. Some have diagrams in which the position of the follicle in the ovaries is shaded to indicate its exact position and size, while others achieve a similar result by using a system of letters and figures combined. The diameter of the follicle is nearly always recorded in centimetres rather than in inches.

Owners often ask whether such examinations achieve the objects for which they are intended and whether they are really necessary. A simple answer is not easily given. Taking the figures quoted in the annual returns of the General Stud Book, it can certainly be argued that the examinations have not reduced the number of twins born or aborted each year, nor have they produced any spectacular rise in the percentage of mares conceiving. Another puzzling feature is the fact that, despite the widespread habit of ovarian palpation, the number of mares covered each year by the leading stallions has remained roughly the same - 40 to 50 per horse - which is the same now as it was 20 or 30 years ago, when the practice of palpating ovaries was not in vogue.

So, despite the fact that we are now able to reduce the number of services that stallions are required to give to their mares during each season, such success has not been used to very good effect by the industry in its effort to ensure that the best sire lines serve more mares, perhaps 60 to 70 a year. There is a popular belief, unsupported by any biological evidence, that the more services given by a horse the shorter will be his working life.

There can be little doubt, despite the national statistics, that many individual mares are helped to conceive and are cured of infertility as a result of the examinations that have been described. This fact, together with their undoubted usefulness as a management tool in the day-to-day mating programme of a stud is probably sufficient justification for them.

Modern veterinary science should never be used as a means of taking a short-cut across the well-established principles of sensible breeding policy, which must be based on the selection of healthy stock, with the rigorous elimination of bad character traits by the simple process of culling undesirables.

13: Diagnosis of pregnancy

The diagnosis as to whether or not a mare is pregnant can be very helpful to the thoroughbred breeding industry. It is not so long ago that buyers at sales necessarily had to guess by the size of a mare whether or not she was pregnant. Nowadays it is customary to have certificates stating that the animal has been examined and found to be pregnant within a short period prior to the sale.

Once a mare becomes pregnant she will remain permanently out of season until after the foal is born. For instance, if a mare comes into oestrus on 1 March and this lasts until 5 March, she might be expected to return on the 22 March. If, however, she is mated and becomes pregnant she will not again show in season. Although a few mares, when pregnant, may show outward signs that could be taken as indicating that they are in use, they will rarely, if ever, accept the stallion. If all mares showed this typical behaviour we would only have to observe if they were in season after mating at 21 days to know whether or not they were pregnant, with no need for veterinary diagnosis. Unfortunately, given the rather artificial conditions under which mares are bred in this country, they may show very marked deviations from typical behaviour.

Having been covered in early March, a mare which has not conceived, may in fact fail to come into oestrus for several weeks or even months. In extreme cases, they might remain out of oestrus until the end of the covering season on 15 July. Alternatively, they may go six or nine weeks, so that valuable time is lost before a successful mating can take place. A pregnancy test during the stud season can therefore be a very useful aid to those concerned with the mating of mares.

By determining that a mare is barren at any stage after she has once been mated, the stud groom is alerted to the fact that the mare is 'cheating' at the trying board if she fails to show signs of oestrus for long periods of time. It also allows the vet to apply treatment in an attempt to bring the mare back into a normal sexual cycle so that she may be covered and got in foal. The vet can palpate the uterus during a rectal examination and feel for changes that occur as a result of pregnancy. By about Day 19 following conception, the uterus is felt as a firm Y-shaped organ. A small bulge may in some cases be felt at the junction of the uterine horn and body where the foetus takes up position. This bulge increases in size until it is readily identifiable at about Day 40. The accuracy of pregnancy testing by this method increases considerably over the early stages of pregnancy. Before the advent of ultrasound scanning, a positive certification by the vet of pregnancy was not usually given before Day 40 because of the problem of being absolutely sure that rectal examination was accurate prior to this stage.

Echography (scanning) is a relatively new technique in veterinary medicine. The principle behind this technique is the same as that employed in the detection of underwater objects, such as submarines. Sound waves of very high frequency (2-7 mHZ) are transmitted outwards from an electrode or transducer. These sound waves

are reflected wherever there is a change of texture between two surfaces. For example, the waves are carried through water but when encountering a solid object or a change from one type of fluid to another, varying amounts of the sound waves are reflected in a backwards direction. These waves are then picked up by the same transducer that emitted the original signal and transformed into a visual display. This display can be interpreted in terms of the size, shape and nature of the 'object' through which the ultrasound waves are passing. Ultrasound scanning is now a routine aid to veterinary examinations of a mare's genital organs prior to mating or for the purpose of pregnancy diagnosis.

A method of testing for pregnancy which does not involve rectal examination or scanning is one in which a blood sample may be examined between Day 45 and Day 100 of pregnancy. During this time a large amount of hormone known as eCG (equine chorionic gonadotrophin), once known as PMSG (pregnant mare's serum gonadotrophin) circulates in the mare's blood. This hormone is produced in the uterus by small ulcer-like structures that form between the foetal membranes and the uterine wall. These are known as endometrial cups. Until fairly recently, the blood could be injected into rabbits, mice or frogs under controlled laboratory conditions and a diagnosis of pregnancy was made on the basis of certain changes observed in these animals after a few days. However, nowadays the blood may be subjected to a special test based on an immune reaction conducted in a test tube (Rapi Tex PMSG, Behring, Marburg, Germany). If the result is positive (ie if the hormone is present in the mare's bloodstream), the mare may be considered to be pregnant and, if not, she is non-pregnant or barren. The blood test is reliable between Day 45 and Day 90 when the endometrial cups disappear to a natural process of resolution.

Another method of pregnancy testing is by means of a chemical test on the mare's urine. This involves the detection of large quantities of oestrogen hormone present in the pregnant mare's urine after about Day 130 of pregnancy. This test is reliable from this time until the foal is born. Because it is only useful after the fourth month of pregnancy, it has no value during the stud season.

For the purposes of sale a positive diagnosis of pregnancy is obviously of great value, but during the stud season it is a negative result which is looked for. Because of the possible loss of the foetus in the early stages of pregnancy, it is always advisable to re-test the animal that is found to be pregnant. The earlier the diagnosis the more important to re-test at a later date. If the mare is found to be in foal early in the season, re-testing at nine weeks and even again at twelve weeks - if it is before the end of June - is advisable in order to make sure that the pregnancy is continuing normally.

When a mare is examined by ultrasound or rectal examination and found not to be in foal, the problem of how to induce her to return to season, once a most difficult problem, has now been resolved by the availability of the drug prostaglandin. This stops the yellow body from producing progesterone and the

mare naturally comes back into oestrous.

There is a natural loss of early pregnancies from the moment of conception onwards. In practice this means that a mare identified as being in foal by any method at 19 days or more from the last mating may fail to produce a foal. With the use of ultrasound scanning the timing of this loss can be identified very accurately. A mare examined at, say, 20 days and then again at 27 days may be found to be pregnant upon the first occasion and not in foal on the second occasion. Alternatively, the foetus may be seen to be in a dying state on the second occasion and it is possible in such circumstances to predict its loss within a few days.

Once the hormone eCG is produced in the uterus at Day 37 to 40, it is unusual to be able to stimulate a mare to return to a fertile oestrous until such time as the eCG hormone has cleared from the bloodstream. This occurs at about Day 120 from conception. This knowledge is particularly important to the manner in which we deal with twins, as discussed in the next chapter.

14: Twins in the thoroughbred

Twins are regarded with great dismay by many owners because they are very often aborted, or else, having been carried to full-term, are rarely an economic proposition due to their small size. Furthermore, mares that slip twins are sometimes more difficult to get in foal the following breeding season.

The reason for this poor outcome for twins in horses is because of the unique disposition of the equine placenta. In species other than those belonging to the family of horses, the placenta is attached to a part only of the wall of the uterus. There is therefore room for two or more membranes to exist side by side. In the horse, the placenta is spread over the whole surface of the uterus and a second membrane therefore causes competition for attachment to the uterine wall. The result of this competition is that both membranes become damaged, although one may grow at the expense of the other. This variation depends on the area which one placental membrane can achieve relative to the other. In many instances, there may be a fifty-fifty split. In this case, one might expect two half-sized foals to be born at full-term. In practice this may occur but more often the damage done by one placenta to the other during its competition for space results in one or both of the twins dying. The pregnancy then ends in abortion or the birth of one foal that is dead and one that may have some chance of living but which is usually much smaller than the normal birthweight. About 5 per cent of thoroughbred mares conceive twins but pony breeds seldom do so.

Ultrasound scanning has made it possible to diagnose twinning at an early stage in many instances. Using ultrasound, twins may be identified as early as 12 days from conception, although most vets make an examination at around 17 days when the 'black hole' appearance of the conceptus is sufficiently large to enable them to distinguish it more readily from a cyst. Each conceptus may lie side by side or one in each horn of the uterus. If the twins are separate one of them may be readily squeezed and eliminated at the 17 day stage. This operation is performed by the veterinary surgeon leaving the other twin to continue normally as a singleton pregnancy. If the twins are lying side-by-side, squeezing is not so effective because it often ends in both members of the twin being eliminated. One of the advantages of pregnancy diagnosis made earlier than 17 days is that the conceptus is not usually attached to the uterine wall at that stage and gentle massaging by the veterinary surgeon may separate one twin from the other, thereby providing the opportunity for one or other of the twins to be squeezed and eliminated.

Ultrasound scanning for pregnancy diagnosis provides a very accurate means for identifying the loss of the embryo at any particular stage that it occurs. Many pregnancies are lost between Day 17 and 30 or between Day 30 and 40, for example. Before scanning, early diagnoses were not sufficiently accurate for pregnancy loss to be identified with any certainty.

15: Problem of barren mares

It must be stressed that there are many causes of barrenness. The problem of infertility in mares is basically a problem of individuals, although occasionally there is a problem of mass infertility resulting from sterility of the stallion, the spread of infection amongst brood mares in a localised community, or nutritional or other managerial errors. Fortunately the causes of epidemic infertility are infrequently encountered and are usually limited to relatively small numbers by the nature of the multitude of small units of which the horse breeding industry is composed.

While every effort must be made to treat individual cases on their merits, this is only possible when there is continuity of approach and a reliable history from one season to the next. Sometimes a mare arrives at a stud farm at the beginning of the season with little or no information regarding her breeding history or the problems from which she has suffered during the preceding 12 months. The stud groom and vet are then in a position of having to find out the particular difficulties of the mare from scratch. In this way, valuable time is often lost and the proper assessment of the ways in which the mare might be given help to effect conception is delayed, or her chances lost completely. The terms 'sexual cycle' and 'sexual behaviour' denote that there is a pattern to the sex life of a mare. This pattern cannot be assessed by one examination or one observation alone, whether by a vet or the stud groom. To come to grips with the problem in any individual, it is always necessary to view it over a period of time, just as it takes a moving and not a still film to tell us in which direction a mountaineer is moving on a rock face.

It is natural for mares to breed and it is as well for everyone to remember this truism. There is, however, a marked divergence of opinion amongst owners as to how far they will accept the corollary that it is also natural for mares to go barren from time to time, and even to become permanently sterile.

Just how much effort should be put into trying to increase the fertility rate depends very much on how these two extremes are viewed. Those that are content to leave events entirely to nature must bear in mind that the thoroughbred, in this country at least, is bred under unnatural conditions and the consequences of these conditions are bound to depress the fertility rate well below that which would be expected in a natural habitat. Given this, it is always a temptation for disappointed owners to place the blame upon the shoulders of the stud groom, which is certainly unfair. 'Why hasn't my mare come in season and been covered?' is a question often asked as the stud season progresses. At the present time, it is sufficient to say that it is erroneous to assume that nature will always provide the right answers, especially under the artificial environment in which we keep the thoroughbred.

The great majority of owners have now come to accept the fact that their financial interests are best served by making every effort to obtain conception in every case and, in this way, to try to do better than the national average. This has, of course, entailed a greater degree of unnatural control aimed solely at looking for the potentially barren mare in any one season.

In other words, if we reckon that there is a three-to-one chance that a mare will not conceive in any year, the task must be to spot that mare in time, and help her in such a way that she 'beats the book'. In order to achieve this, it is necessary to examine the other three mares very carefully and this has naturally led to opposition from the 'naturalists'. However, opportunities for thoroughbred mares to roam over wide areas of country unmolested by human interference, while a pleasant thought, is not a practicable proposition.

To meet the views of the naturalists we must therefore listen to any particular objection to the measures conventionally employed and, in the light of the information available, assess whether or not more harm than good is done in any particular way. For instance, the merit of pregnancy examinations at an early stage has been widely debated, but there is no evidence that early rectal palpation, in itself, causes abortion. Therefore, the advantages that the industry obtains from such examinations during the stud season should not be dispensed with because of criticism in some quarters. However, criticisms should be aired and discussed fully without fear or favour by all concerned in the industry. There is a great need for detailed information on which to base constructive thought and debate, and there is much room within the industry for better tabulation of data, not only to enable individual mares to be better cared for at the studs, but also so that the aggregate of information can be accumulated for the benefit of the industry as a whole. A number of surveys have been carried out in recent years to ascertain the prevalence of venereal infection in the mare and stallion population. Other surveys have resulted from work conducted by organisations such as the TBA Fertility Unit with a view to improving methods of controlling the oestrous cycle by drugs and other means.

Among the causes of infertility, the part played by infection is an important one. When infection is said to be a cause of infertility, that generally means an infection of the uterus. The infection is localised in the uterus and does not cause a general ailment or illness in the mare. The result of bacteria breeding in the uterus has two main effects. Firstly, it seriously reduces the length of life of the spermatozoa and thus lessens the chance of conception occurring. Secondly, if conception does in fact occur, it lessens the chance of survival of the fertilised egg, so that it may fail to develop within the uterus and subsequently be aborted. In severe infections, adhesions may form at the cervix within the uterus, or in the fallopian tubes. In the latter case, the ducts may become blocked, so preventing the passage of the egg into the uterus.

The uterus has a dual function. At one end it receives the egg, while at the other it is continuous with the outside, through the cervix so that the sperm may be deposited within it. Once conception has occurred, however, it has to function as a closed organ in which the foetus can develop for 11 months. The first function necessarily increases the risk of infection being introduced, just as with any other organ that communicates with the outside.

The defence mechanisms of the uterus against infection consist of the secretions from the walls within the uterus, the capacity of the cervix to open and shut at the appropriate times, and the structure of the vagina and vulva, which are so composed that they normally prevent air from going into the tract, taking with it bacteria and other infective agents.

There are two types of infection of the mare's genital tract, namely those caused by non-specific microbes such as streptococcus, *E coli* and those caused by specific venereal germs, namely contagious equine metritis organism (CEMO), Klebsiella and pseudomonas. The streptococcus is a very common organism found in damaged tissue, and *E coli* is found in abundance within the environment of the mare, being a normal bacterium in faeces. When these and other similar microbes are present in uterine infection they are probably playing a role secondary to some other condition, such as air being sucked abnormally into the genital tract or as a result of a chronic degeneration of the defence mechanisms of the genital tract, particularly in an older mare. CEMO and the other two venereal microbes have a special place, because they are particularly virulent organisms which once established in the uterus can cause a great deal of damage and which are very difficult to eliminate. They do not necessarily require conditions which allow them to become established in the uterus but may invade even healthy tissues.

Contagious equine metritis (CEM) was first reported among mares on stud farms in the Newmarket area during 1977. It had previously been an unrecognised disease. Signs included a copious discharge from the vagina and the condition was highly contagious. The cause of the disease was eventually identified as an organism which is now known as *Taylorensis equigenitalis*, named after Dr Taylor of Addenbrooke's Hospital, Cambridge, whose laboratory made the first identification. The disease was found in other large breeding centres and a scientific committee was established by the Horserace Betting Levy Board in an effort to control the spread of the infection. This committee published a Code of Practice which contained a number of recommendations aimed at controlling the disease during the 1978 breeding season. These recommendations are still in force today, although they have been updated on an annual basis. They involve a screening programme for mares and stallions based on examinations for the presence of bacteria on the penis of the stallion and in the genital tract of the mare. It is a tribute to the effectiveness of the recommendations that the disease has largely disappeared from thoroughbreds worldwide, although it is still present in some non-thoroughbred breeds.

Klebsiella infection is also much less common, probably due to the programme of swabbing of the genital tract of mares for the presence of this and other bacteria, now commonly practised routinely. There are many different strains of Klebsiella and only a few are harmful. These are numbered according to their outer layer, or capsule, as capsullar types 1, 3 and 5.

Pseudomonas is a more capricious microbe and although it is quite commonly encountered its harmfulness is not apparently as certain as that of Klebsiella or CEMO. These three types of bacteria are truly venereal in the sense that they may spread in epidemic form from one mare to another via the stallion. Unlike venereal disease in man, the male is rarely affected but carries the germ on his penis or in the smegma of the sheath and transmission occurs during coitus so that once an infected mare has been mated with a stallion he may pass the infection to other mares.

The prime method of preventing venereal spread is to screen mares and stallions for the presence of venereal microbes and to avoid mating until such time as treatment has cleared the infection. This is more readily achieved in some instances than in others, depending on the severity and extent of the infection in the mare's genital tract or on the surface of the stallion's penis.

The development of an infection in the mare's uterus depends upon the nature and virulence of the infecting germ. Virulence denotes the capacity to infect and invade tissue. We have already discussed how three venereal germs have the ability to invade and set up an infection whereas others require some help from diminished resistance on the part of a host. Such diminished resistance is particularly associated with mares recovering from the effects of foaling, age and poor conformation of the genital tract which allows the entry of air.

There are three primary means of identifying infection in the mare. The first is to collect small samples of mucous from the cervix of the mare when she is in heat. This is the method of the so-called cervical swab. The sample is placed in special transport medium in a swab casing and transported to the laboratory. In the laboratory, it is smeared on a dish containing special media for incubation at blood temperature for 24-48 h. The bacteria, if present, grow and can be identified by staining and other means of biochemical testing. Swab material may also be taken to make a smear on a slide by which cells in the mucous can be examined under a microscope. The presence of PMNs (polymorphonuclear leucocytes) or pus cells indicate that inflammation is present, a cardinal sign of infection.

The third means of identifying infection is to take a small pinch of lining from the uterus by means of a biopsy punch. This is a long rod with small jaws at one end and a handle at the other. The instrument is inserted into the uterus and the jaws close over a small piece of lining. After clamping the jaws and thereby capturing the specimen, the instrument is removed and the sample taken into special fluids in preparation for staining at the laboratory and the making of sections which can be examined under the microscope. The exact health status of the uterine lining can then be examined by the pathologist and a report given as to whether or not infection or other abnormal changes are present. Swabs may also be taken from the clitoris and this is a particularly useful means of screening mares for the three venereal microbes. A whole host of other microbes may be present in the clitoris but these are not regarded as being of any significance.

16: Treatment of infertility

The chance of a successful conception occurring to any service by the stallion depends, as we have seen, on the survival of the spermatozoa in the mare until the egg is shed at the time of ovulation. Once the latter occurs, the chance of conception is reduced to zero during the following 24 hours. The ideal time of service is therefore about 12 hours before ovulation occurs. The longer the sperm are deposited in the uterus before ovulation, the less chance there is that conception will occur. The manual examination of ovaries by rectal palpation is therefore a valuable aid in the management of mares and in deciding the best time at which mating should occur.

As we have previously seen, the factors which affect the length of life of the sperm within the uterus depend on the conditions within that organ and to some extent on the quality of semen produced by the stallion. Conditions in the uterus are adversely affected by infection and quite possibly by hormonal imbalance leading to secretions in the uterus which are not conducive to sperm survival. Rectal palpation is therefore more important in mares in which there are abnormal conditions in the uterus than in the healthy, normally functioning ones. This type of mare is often known as a 'difficult' one.

The custom of covering mares in each heat period with a day, or possibly two days, between each service, might well advantageously be replaced by services on two successive days on those occasions when a veterinary examination shows the mare to have the optimum chance of conceiving - if, for example, there is a good follicle present in the ovary, and the uterus, vagina and so on appeared in a healthy condition. By covering twice in 24 hours, the chances of putting the sperm into the uterus at the very best time with regard to the point of ovulation, and in additional quantities, naturally gives a better chance of conception in 'difficult' mares.

Infertility is not treated merely by injecting a hormone or washing out the uterus with an antibiotic. It involves a study of the mare over a long period and through several heat periods in order to diagnose the likely cause of trouble. The time to start considering what should be done to help a barren mare is during the months outside the stud season. For instance, treatment of the uterus when it is infected requires a period of sexual rest. During the stud season the results of treatment are often spoiled by the necessity of having the mare covered too soon.

The importance of tabulating the behaviour pattern and the sex cycles of mares needs stressing. Detailed year-to-year notes regarding the abnormalities and functioning of the genital organs of the individual mare are extremely helpful to the vet, providing as they do clues to the reasons for infertility. He regards this information as clues in his search for the reasons for infertility. To be worthwhile records should be simple and accurate. Such background knowledge of the past is essential if help in achieving conception is to be provided. Although a table is not intended to be the last word on the manner in which information is recorded, the writer believes that an agreed *pro forma* should be accepted by breeders in their own interests. Progress depends on veterinary surgeons and horse owners co-operating in the compilation of statistical information on which research can be based. The idea of record sheets for mares could well be extended to other classes of animals such as foals, yearlings, horses in training, and so on, with valuable results.

For instance, if we wished to know whether there was a relationship between inheritance and arthritis of the knees or between certain foal diseases and a failure to stand training, continuous record sheets subjected to statistical analysis would eventually answer the question. Although a 'mare record sheet' might be regarded by some as so much red tape, the writer suggests that the trouble involved in its completion by breeders would be effort spent in their own interests.

Finally, what is the effect of age on the fertility of a mare?

Age is a process affecting every living creature. Old age does not happen suddenly. It is a gradual wearing down of the various parts of the body until, at last, a vital organ ceases to function and death of the whole organism results. In the mare, as in other animals, the breeding organs usually cease to function sometime before termination of the life span of the individual.

The age at which any particular mare ceases to breed varies considerably. Some may not breed after the age of 15, while others bear foals in the mid-twenties. We cannot, therefore, regard age as a specific cause of infertility, but only one that predisposes the failure of some part of the breeding organs for any one of the reasons already discussed, such as infection or glandular disorder. It is possible that we could increase the length of the breeding life of mares by paying more attention to inherited tendencies such as faulty conformation of the genital tract and reduced breeding potential. Selection of breeding stock purely on the grounds of racing ability is not always consistent with high fertility and a prolonged life span.

The basis of all treatment is the diagnosis of the cause of the condition which is being dealt with. For instance, the treatment of infection, whether it is in the uterus or elsewhere in the body, depends on knowledge of the reason for the presence of the infection and the nature of the organism which is causing the infection, together with its sensitivity to the various drugs which are available to us. Hormonal or glandular imbalance can only be treated if we know which hormone or which gland is at fault and why.

17: How to improve the breed

In an article in *The Sporting Life* entitled 'A healthy crisis is on the way', John Hislop suggested that a recession in the industry would improve the standard of the breed, by forcing owners to eliminate stock.

He went on to suggest that, if breeding stock were to be reduced by as much as 50 per cent, only the best retained, and wastage kept to a minimum, the breed as a whole and owners individually, would benefit.

Veterinary surgeons would tend to agree. However, the problem of deciding which stock is best and which should be discharged, remains. Mating by pedigree is very helpful, as it provides a label to the material that is being used, so that there is a purposeful selection through many generations rather than a system whereby matings are arranged by pure chance.

The grounds on which selection is made are crucial. Performance on the racecourse is one obvious factor, as, too, are those physical factors we describe as conformation, toughness, and so on. However, what is the underlying identity behind such vague generalisations? Tendencies towards arthritis, fractures and sprains, for example, are eliminated only by breeding horses with the necessary 'hardness' in the structures involved. Again, the size of the heart, the efficiency of the circulation and the lungs, are all part of a horse's ability and toughness.

While many ills suffered by horses arise from management rather than from inheritance, there is nonetheless ample evidence that adverse structural defects can be perpetuated and increased within the breed by injudicious mating. It is important to be watchful to ensure a good balance of qualities to produce the best kind of horse for racing purposes.

The starting point for a campaign of reduction and avoidance of waste might first be directed at the actual capacity of the breeding stock to produce live foals. Figures from the General Stud Book of 1964 show that out of 8,710 mares who were covered by stallions, 2,571 (29.5 per cent) were returned as barren. If the returns over the years are examined, it is apparent that 29.5 per cent is a rough average figure. In 1916, it was 27.5 per cent, in 1947, 33 per cent, while in the arctic weather of 1963 it was 29.35 per cent, a proportion which seems to indicate that, rain or shine, the average fertility of mares in this country remains much the same from one year to another.

It is only possible to guess at the annual financial loss to the bloodstock industry from such failure to achieve conception in so many individuals. In the nineties, there has been an improvement but with a 25% barren figure and an average of £5,000 per head in a population of 10,000 mares the loss to cover the cost of keep, nominations, insurance, transport, etc suggests a waste of approximately £12.5m. This total does not include loss arising from mares becoming pregnant and subsequently aborting, having dead foals or giving birth to foals that die in the first week of life. Nor does it include the rather intangible loss caused by the waste in man hours involved in trying and covering to no avail. Nor the loss to stallion owners of potential progeny which would successfully advertise their sires on the racecourse.

Could modern science and modern methods have done more to improve fertility? If the figures seem bad, it should be appreciated that the number of mares covered in each year has increased by more than half between 1916 and 1964; in 1916, 5,299 mares were covered, in 1964 the figure was 8,710. In 1992 it was 19,597. That an almost constant proportion of barren to pregnant mares has been maintained, despite this large increase, may actually reflect a relative success, for it is reasonable to have expected the proportion to increase as greater numbers were involved. Good results are more easy to achieve, the smaller the group.

UK figures compare favourably with those of other countries so, if there is no cause for congratulation, nor is there for despair.

Breeders of ponies generally obtain a much higher fertility in their breeding stock due to their willingness to breed in the natural breeding season, rather than to impose an arbitrary time limit to the mating season, as is the case with thoroughbred studs. Also, ponies that are difficult to breed are usually quickly eliminated and not subjected to intensive measures of stud and veterinary management. There is therefore less likelihood of the selection of pony breeding stock to be biased towards infertility, as may inadvertently be occurring in thoroughbreds. In fact, the application of modern methods of stud management may be camouflaging an actual increase of undesirable inherited characteristics as far as fertility is concerned. There may, in the near future, for this reason, be a dramatic fall in fertility rates as modern methods become inadequate to hold the position against unconscious selection for infertility.

Of the 2,500 or so mares which are annually barren, there is a hard core which shuffles round in succeeding years to different stallions, each year arriving at the studs with fresh hope, each year leaving empty or occasionally conceiving and producing a live foal, but often subsequently aborting. The 'blessing' of a 'no foal, no fee' arrangement facilitates and prolongs the life of these individuals. These mares are often infected and their continual return to the stallion thereby endangers other mares visiting the same horse. A sensible method of reducing this band of hopefuls is by raising the rates of keep and nominations, so that bad breeders are penalised and good ones subsidised - a tax on services, a rebate for production!

The exact proportion of barrenness due to infection is not known on a national scale.

18: Breeding thoroughbreds

The business of breeding thoroughbreds calls for a constant vigil 24 hours a day, seven days a week. During the early months of the year when the 'stud season' is in full swing there are just two objectives: to deliver the previous year's crop of foals and to mate the mares with the stallions, so laying the foundation of the next year's crop. To this end, about 40 mares per stallion are collected on the various studs where the stallions are kept. Many of these public studs, as they are called, have two or more stallions and all the animals have to be housed, fed and cared for in every way.

In contrast to an industry based on the product of man's own invention, such as machinery, the bloodstock breeding industry must necessarily conform to the rule set for it by nature. The pattern of work is therefore determined by the way the horses sleep, eat, breed and exercise. Those who work in the industry are therefore required at all times to adapt themselves to meet these requirements.

Where should one begin a description of a 24-hour day? Let us start at the point when many are locking their office doors and going home. At six in the evening, the stud groom, or one of his assistants, is making his round, looking at each animal on the stud. As he goes from box to box he takes particular note of the pregnant mares, looking at each individual for signs that her time of labour may be near. It is considered essential that all births should be supervised, in case there is trouble at this time. To allow a mare to foal without anyone present is one of the deadliest sins that can be committed by a stud. The stud groom knows that most mares give birth between 6pm and 6am and, although the event must be expected at any time, it is much more likely to occur during that period.

The groom already has a rough idea on which day the mare may be expected to foal. The date is calculated as 11 months from the last service during the previous year, but as it is quite normal for a mare to give birth at least three weeks on either side of that time, he must always be on his guard. A more reliable guide is the development of the two mammary glands, or udder, of the mare. These normally increase in size two or three weeks before she produces her foal while a few days prior to the event the glands will fill with milk, which may, in some cases, be seen dripping from the teats. In addition, a wax-like substance often appears at the end of each teat 24 to 48 hours before foaling occurs. 'Bagging-up' is the phrase often used in the trade for this process! Other tell-tale signs that birth is imminent include a lengthening of the vulva, a depression over the quarters as the ligaments relax, restlessness and an increase in skin temperature felt over the neck and shoulders, associated perhaps with an outbreak of patchy sweating. The latter signs are referred to as warming up and the birth may be expected to start in hours, if not minutes.

The stud groom next goes to the mares that have already had their foals. He will want to see if the foal has been sucking regularly from the mare. Normally the foal will feed at frequent intervals from its mother, perhaps every half-hour, but if it does not do so the udder will become full of milk and the teats tense. After an hour or two the udder will be felt as being firm or even hard and milk may stream out of the teats and down the legs of the mare. On the other hand, if the foal has recently sucked, the udder will be soft and the teats slack and moistened with saliva.

Signs of distress and illness in the foal can be seen in the way it lies, the rate of breathing and the manner in which it gets to its feet when disturbed. Symptoms of diarrhoea will be noticed under the tail and on the buttocks.

From the mares and foals, the stud groom's round next takes him to the barren mares who, until April, are stabled at night but thereafter they may be found in the paddocks running out day and night. Here again the stud groom notes if there are any signs of discomfort, whether one mare is by herself, perhaps rolling with pain, or maybe lame. He looks to see if the stabled mares have eaten their evening feed, the number of dungs in their box, or if the straw bedding has been disturbed, as might well happen if a mare has been rolling or scraping the ground with colic.

At 8pm or thereabouts, the night watchman, or sitting-up man as he is usually called in this country, takes up his duties. He makes similar rounds to those described above. Through the hours of the night, he is responsible for alerting the stud groom at the first sign of trouble or impending birth. He must be alert for any circumstance and must not sleep. A not infrequent occurrence on a stud is for a mare or foal to become cast against the side of the box, so that it is unable to get up from the ground without help.

Illness may strike at any time, such as when a mare gets colic, or a foal shows itself to be ill by 'going off suck'. When trouble arises and appears to be of a serious nature, the vet is called. It may also be necessary to call upon another studsman so that the sitting-up man may be freed for his normal duties.

Nowadays, most stud farms have television monitors in each foaling box. These relay pictures to monitors placed in sitting-up rooms and/or in the stud groom's house. The monitors can be set to relay the pictures in sequence from box to box or be left to play on one loose box, according to the need of the moment.

The closeness of a mare to foaling may also be gauged by taking small samples of milk from the udder and testing these for calcium content. When a mare is close to foaling, the calcium content of the colostrum increases five- to ten-fold. Special tests with strips that change colour according to the calcium content are a useful aid, especially on small stud farms where sitting-up nightly presents a problem.

The stud groom is informed immediately a mare shows signs that she is about to foal. If all goes well, there may be very little for him to do but he must be present to make sure that labour is proceeding in a normal and satisfactory manner. He may ease the foetus from the mother as she delivers it, put antiseptic dressings on the navel stump, tie up the afterbirth behind the mare and, when this drops, remove it from the box for burial. He may dry the newborn foal with a cloth and hold the mare once the foal is on its feet and assist it in the search it instinctively makes for its mother's udder. He may administer an enema of liquid paraffin or soap and water to help the passing of the foetal dung (meconium). During these duties he will keep a careful watch to note any signs that all is not well with the foal or the mare. He knows that the mare will often show evidence of pain as her uterus contracts but, if too violent or prolonged, it may mean that haemorrhage is occurring from the blood vessels supplying her uterus.

Perhaps two hours after the birth the stud groom can retire to bed but, in the height of the season (March and April), when the number of foalings are at their maximum, he may well be called again. The closest watch of all has to be kept on the newborn foals during their first three days of life. It is during this time that most trouble tends to occur, from retained meconium, ruptured bladders, haemolytic diseases, septicaemia and a host of other ills, the early signs of which must be spotted in order to give the vet a proper chance to treat and cure.

As dawn breaks, the main staff appear and the rituals of the day begin. The animals are fed with corn or nuts, and the barren mares and those that have already foaled are taken one by one to the presence of an entire horse, known as a teaser (as explained in Chapter 11).

Then, if the weather is suitable, the mares are turned into the paddocks while at some time the vet will arrive to examine the mares that are in oestrus. These examinations have become standard practice on most of the big studs of Great Britain and Ireland. In this way the stud manager, stud groom and vet work closely together in deciding which mares are forward enough to justify them being covered on any particular day. Also the mares that do not genuinely show to the teaser or which cheat will be inspected to see if they are, in fact, in oestrus. Some mares may need treatment before they can be mated to give them a greater chance of conception. In this way each day, mares are selected for mating and then led to a special yard known as the covering yard, usually found close to where the stallions are stabled. This is often some distance from the main part of the stud where the mares are kept. At the height of the stud season the stallion will cover two or, possibly three, mares during the day, with an interval of perhaps only a few hours between each. At other times, however, it may be that none of his mares will be in oestrus, or ready for mating.

Every morning, the loose boxes have to be cleaned out. The soiled bedding is removed, fresh straw and hay supplied, water mangers are cleaned out, and yards and roadways swept clean. In the afternoon, the animals have to be returned to their boxes from the paddocks. In the evening, feed of corn or mash is taken to each box and the animals are hayed for the night. This brings the daily round full circle.

On top of these routine matters, a sick animal requiring nursing may impose a considerable additional burden. One or two men may have to be employed for many hours to help the vet by holding or nursing a sick animal.

For those who work on studs, tied as they are to the natural habits of the horse in its artificial surroundings, the line of demarcation between leisure and work is not easily drawn.

19: Pregnancy and the mare

As icy winds sweep across the countryside, so the thoroughbred breeding season gets under way! From January to June, the results of the previous matings arrive in ever-increasing numbers. Of the total, the largest percentage of foals will be born during March and April.

In persuading our mares to give birth during the first three months of the year, at a time quite against their natural inclination, do we in fact take enough precautions to offset the disadvantages to their offspring? The latter, while barely 18 months of age, will be used, not only as a beast of burden with 120lb or more of man and saddle on its back, but also, by the time it is two years of age, to travel with the same burden at full gallop. Against this background of excessive and premature demands, the time spent within the uterus is seen to be of immense relative importance. It is surely the period to 'make or break' the individual.

The struggle for existence begins from the very moment of conception and it is as well for horse owners constantly to bear in mind the health and safety of the developing foal or foetus at all stages of pregnancy. There are many points at which the new individual can be put at hazard while still in the uterus. Infection of various kinds within the uterus can destroy the foetus at a very early stage. Upsets in hormonal control may seriously interfere with growth and be responsible for death. Twins (as already noted) are rarely carried successfully by a mare because of the competition for a limited amount of placenta, and therefore nourishment, within the uterus.

How does management materially alter the chances of successful development of the foal within the uterus? In considering this problem, it is convenient to divide the duration of pregnancy into three periods.

The individual starts as a single cell, which contains the genetic material which it receives from the parents. This material is not altered in that individual from the time of conception for the rest of its life, except under very exceptional circumstances. As the cell moves down the fallopian tubes into the uterus, it starts a process of division, first into two cells, then into four and so on. The new cells take on specialised roles, so forming the various organs of the body.

In a matter of weeks, a miniature foal an inch or two in length - complete with head, body, limbs, heart, liver and so on - can be recognised. A few features such as the hair do not appear until much later in pregnancy, a fact which reflects the order of priorities. Hair is not essential to the life of the foetus, but only to the foal once it has been expelled from the uterus, when it forms a necessary 'coat' against the cold. On the other hand, organs such as the heart and blood vessels are vital to the life of the foetus from a very early time in pregnancy. This first stage of development, lasting five or six weeks, is often called the embryological period. It is a time of formation rather than growth.

The second stage of pregnancy is one of gradual growth of all parts and the

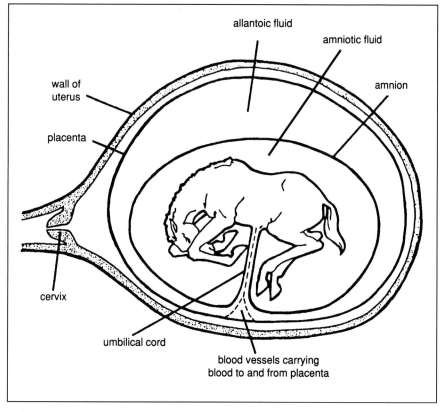

Fig 19.1: The foal inside the uterus

development of the placenta. This latter organ is designed to extract nourishment for the foal from the mother. The placenta also carries out functions such as the elimination of waste material while the foetus is completely enclosed within its mother and thus isolated from the outside world.

The third and final stage occupies about four months of pregnancy preceding birth. During this time, the growth rate of the foetus is very rapid and its size and weight increase enormously. If we measure length at five weeks gestation, we find it is no more than 2in, at 12 weeks about 6-8in, at 24 weeks 28in and at full term 40in. Weight increases correspondingly, from 30lb at six months to 100lb or more at birth.

The appearance of the mother is no guide to the well being of the foetus that she is carrying. The owner of the mare or those who look after her may see a well-nourished, even fat, individual giving no cause for alarm or worry at any stage of pregnancy. But at birth, a miserable under-nourished weakling of a foal may appear, hardly capable perhaps of surviving at all. On the other hand, another mare, poor in

Pregnancy and the mare

condition, can give birth to a healthy, strong and well-nourished foal which causes no concern or difficulties. It is therefore necessary for us to probe deeper before we can begin to appreciate whether or not our methods of management are correct or whether they may be beneficially altered.

It appears that the first and last periods of pregnancy - of formation and of maximum growth - are those in which the foetus can be most easily harmed by incorrect methods. In the first few weeks after conception (the embryological or period of formation), various parts may fail to develop in a proper manner. The foal without eyes, a parrot jaw, a cleft palate or with one leg missing are examples of abnormalities which occur during this period - although we do not see them until the foal is born some ten months later. We have very little knowledge regarding the cause of such defects or 'errors in development' in the horse.

In other species, such as our own, we do know that it may be for one of three reasons. In the first place, they may be due to some defect of the inherited material. It would be quite possible to gather useful information about this factor in the horse if we were able to collect facts relating to the appearance of deformities in various strains of the breed and submit them to statistical analysis. A second possible cause is infection of the mother with viruses which may interfere with the normal development of certain parts of the foetus at the very early stages. The German measles virus in humans, for example, is known to cause deformities. Lastly, a large range of drugs, including thalidomide, have been found to interfere with the normal development of newborn children and animals if given at a very early stage of pregnancy.

In the horse, we have little information as to the number of deformed foals born each year. It is rarely possible to say whether any particular deformity is the result of inheritance, infection or drugs. On general principles, however, it is wise to consider carefully before administering any drug within six or eight weeks of a mare becoming pregnant, in the light of experiences with other species. Not every drug will have a harmful effect but, if it is necessary to give one to the mother during the first two months of pregnancy, the fact should be recorded for future reference. Some people believe deformities in foals are becoming more common but, like so much that is said in the bloodstock world, this may be an impression rather than a fact. The real state of affairs could be usefully monitored.

The last stage of pregnancy is from about the sixth to the eleventh month. During this period the thoroughbred foetus will grow in a dramatic fashion, so that it increases three-fold from a weight of 30lb at about 6 months to some 100-112lb at birth. Owners often ask whether an abortion can be caused by the mare suffering an accident or becoming frightened. Such dramas as the passing of a hunt across land where brood mares are kept or the sound of low flying aircraft are sometimes blamed when subsequent abortions occur. How near to the time of foaling is it safe to move a mare from one stud to another is another question for which an answer is sought. Many mares that abort have no history of having been moved long distances or of being frightened in any way during pregnancy. On the other hand, very many mares travel at all stages of pregnancy by plane, sea and land. Further, many are submitted to disturbing episodes in their environment without any subsequent abortion or apparent ill-effect. There is no absolute answer to such questions. What may be safe for one mare may not be so for another.

A more important question is what factors may harm or retard growth and be the cause of a weak and under-nourished foal with less chance of surviving after birth than should normally be the case. There are certain general principles which must be followed if we are to give the best chance to our pregnant mares, to enable the foals to get the start in life they deserve. Before turning to these it is well to bear in mind that, in the management of animals, we are unlikely to improve on nature and that effort should be directed at eliminating those methods which are antagonistic and detrimental to nature's purposes.

The horse, as a species, has survived longer than man himself and, in bending it to suit his own purposes, man has often fallen into the error of assuming that, at the same time, he can improve its natural body processes (physiology) by human interference. The foetus will develop in the best possible way and have the greatest chance of survival after birth if the mother can live in a natural environment. In altering that environment it is a common conceit to assume that matters are being made better for the mare rather than 'less worse'!

One of the major influences on the foetus is the way in which the mares are fed. The foetus takes priority over the available foodstuffs of the mother, so that if the mother is starved she will sacrifice herself to a great extent. As already noted, the foetus in the last third of pregnancy increases by over 70lb in weight. Its requirements for foodstuffs during this period are therefore enormous relative to those required in the first two-thirds of pregnancy. The additional requirements during the last stage are not so much for carbohydrates or sugar, which supply energy, but for protein. The latter is needed for building muscles and the laying-down of stores of energy to meet the future requirements of the foal when born. The diet of the pregnant mare in the last third of pregnancy must take account of these extra requirements. Here is a point of conflict between practised methods and the requirements of nature. The artificial alteration of the breeding season assures that a high proportion of thoroughbred foals are carried during this last stage of pregnancy at a time when the available protein in the grass is at a minimum. Protein content of pasture is highest in spring, falling steadily in the autumn and sinking usually to its lowest level during winter months. The risk of inadequate supply is also increased according to the severity of the winter. In the average diet of a pregnant mare in this country, hay is virtually the only other source of protein. This is very often of inferior quality, from the protein content point of view, partly due to the bad weather in which it has to be harvested.

It is almost impossible, unless feedstuffs are constantly analysed for protein content, to do more than guess the amount of protein an individual is receiving at any particular time. It would therefore seem advisable to feed pregnant mares a small amount, perhaps only a few ounces, of very high-quality protein, such as is found in dried milk, besides the vitamins and mineral additives which are in popular use. Of course, a balanced diet containing all these substances is necessary if the foetus is to grow normally. It is not known whether those cases of foals born with contracted tendons, for example, are due to dietary imbalances or other factors. Extra protein is necessary not just for the foetus but also to ensure an adequate supply of high-quality mother's milk after the foal has been born. This is especially important for foals born in January and February because of the lack of spring grass available at this time for direct consumption.

Regarding moving mares in the months before they are due to foal, there are certain general principles which dictate the best time to remove the animals from one environment to another. Quite a number of foals are born each year weak and under-nourished at birth. At some stage there has been interference in normal growth and development of the foetus or its placenta, so that the chances of survival at birth are reduced. It is well-known in other species that a dramatic alteration in the environment of the mother, such as extreme changes in diet, temperature, long periods without food, physical injury and upsets of a similar nature, can interfere with the well-being of the foetus without actually killing it. Although these effects may be relatively minor at the time, the damage caused may be sufficient to lead to serious disturbances in the days following birth.

Another important factor which must be taken into account when deciding at what time to send pregnant mares to the studs where they are to foal is the question of immunity or resistance against infectious disease. The newborn foal, unlike infants of our own species, is born with virtually no immunity. It is only after it has fed from its mother and taken the all-important colostrum into its stomach that it receives the immunity conferred by the antibodies contained in this first milk. These antibodies are originally formed in the mother as the result of her contact with the various germs and microbes contained in the particular environment in which she lives. If, therefore, she has been moved to a completely different environment just before foaling, the antibodies that she passes to her foal after its birth may not be the right ones to provide protection.

A simple example may be given of the mare who is sent from the stud where she has had no contact with the influenza cough virus and foals shortly afterwards on premises where this particular strain of germ exists in epidemic form. Her newborn foal receives no influenza antibodies and is thus extremely susceptible to infection. In contrast, another mare who has been present at all times on the second stud and who may earlier have been a victim of the infection, will contain a relatively high level of influenza antibodies in her bloodstream. In this case, she will pass protection to her foal, which will therefore stand a much better chance of avoiding infection. There are other less clear-cut infections than the cited example caused by germs (E coli and others), against which protection can be

Pregnancy and the mare

passed in like manner from mother to offspring.

The foals of recent arrivals can be more susceptible to non-specific conditions such as diarrhoea because the mother has not lived for sufficient time in her new environment to enable her to develop the protective antibody which will be passed to her newborn foal. The time taken for a mare to develop such antibodies in a new environment varies, but in most cases it would be about four weeks.

To sum up, an in-foal mare should be moved at least a month before she foals. As the risk of various upsets or deprivations during the journey will obviously vary according to the method of transport, the distance and so on, and given that these cannot entirely be eliminated, the question remains as to what time these are least likely to interfere with the proper growth of the foetus. The answer can only be found from a properly conducted survey involving sufficient numbers to make comparisons between groups treated in different ways. Without such statistics, it is only possible to say that, in theory, the smaller the foetus and therefore the earlier in pregnancy that a mare is moved, the less the risk involved. Given the rising costs of keeping mares from home, there is a natural inclination of owners to reduce the length of time that their animals are boarded away from home. However, they should at least be aware of the risks if such a policy if carried too far.

20: The birth of a foal

Nothing in nature is quite as dramatic as the change in the way of life of the foetus and the newborn. The foetus dwells in a private pool, whose temperature is thermostatically controlled by the mother, so that there is no problem of keeping itself warm. Nor, in the everyday sense that we know it, does it need to breathe or feed. Oxygen and foodstuffs are supplied by the mother through the placenta which is attached to the wall of the uterus. Similarly, the foetus has little necessity to excrete its own waste material. This is all passed back to the mother through the placenta. What excretion it does perform itself can easily be stored within the membranes surrounding it, or inside the gut, until such time as it can be evacuated after birth.

This sheltered existence lasts throughout pregnancy, which in the horse is about 11 months. During this period of development within the mother, the foetus is completely separated from any contact with the outside world, except through its mother.

The act of birth which terminates pregnancy precipitates the foetus into a way of life which is markedly different from anything it has known before. The actual mechanisms within the body which start the birth process are still something of mystery. Just what controls the length of pregnancy in a given species is a problem which has received much attention from scientists. A number of theories have been put forward, most based on the assumption that some form of hormonal control is involved. A falling level of progesterone, the hormone which prepares the uterus for pregnancy, for instance, is said to trigger the act of birth in some species. Others argue that it is the level of oestrogen in the mother's bloodstream which is the determining factor. Another theory suggests that oxytocin is responsible for putting the mother into labour. Oxytocin is a hormone which comes from the pituitary gland and acts on the muscles of the uterus, causing them to contract.

The hormonal system which initiates birth is complex and may be likened to a series of switches operating in sequence. The two glands in the foetus which play a central role are the pituitary and the cortex (outer layer) of the adrenal gland. These become active in late pregnancy resulting in an increased production of cortisol (cortisone). Cortisol affects many body functions, its overall action being a maturing one. It switches on enzymes associated with hormone production generally and of progesterone, oestrogen and prostaglandin in particular. Cortisol may therefore be regarded as the primary switch preparing the foetal foal for birth and initiating the event itself.

From what source do the significant changes in blood hormone level arise? Does the mother or the foetus control the date at which pregnancy shall end? Various theories have been put forward, based on information from different species. In the mare, it is known that the level of progesterone in the blood is highest during the early months of pregnancy, but after about the fourth month this hormone disappears from the mother's blood. This is due to the fact that it is no longer produced by the ovaries after the fourth month, at which point it is being secreted only by the placenta.

For various reasons progesterone does not pass from the placenta into the mother's bloodstream, but is retained in the foal's circulation only. Because the placenta produces progesterone it might be thought that it is this organ in the mare which controls the time that birth will start. If this were so, however, it would certainly not be through the action of progesterone because the levels in the blood circulating in the foal at birth are still very high. Information collected from the mating of horses and donkeys suggests that it is the composition of the foetus and its tissues which controls the length of pregnancy, not the mare herself. In the present state of knowledge, it is not possible to be at all certain about the exact mechanism which decides when a mare will give birth to her foal.

Whatever determines the length of pregnancy, in practice 11 months in the mare is only a rough guide. No one is surprised if a foal is born two or even three weeks before or after the expected date, as calculated from the last service. If the foal arrives before 11 months, it is usual to label it premature and (less commonly) if it is late, as post-mature. A foal four or five weeks premature is not expected to live. If it is born before that time, the act of birth will probably be described as an abortion. The length of pregnancy, however, is not always a reliable guide to the state of maturity of a foal when born.

Birth is a natural process and, in the great majority of cases, the mare is quite

Fig 20.1: Delivery of a foal, which is enclosed in a fine membrane called the amnion

The birth of a foal

capable of producing a live foal without injury to herself or her foetus. If the foetus is fully mature and healthy, it is unlikely that it will be put at risk in its passage from the uterus to the outside world. By about the sixth or seventh month of pregnancy, the developing foal will have taken up a position with its head facing towards the cervix and its hindquarters towards the mare's chest. From this time until birth, it will lie on its back with the head and forelimbs flexed. As the uterus contracts at the beginning of the birth process, so the pressures within the organ cause the foal to rotate, so that it then lies with its back uppermost. The forelimbs and head extend at the same time and the foal enters the mare's birth canal in the characteristic position of birth - with the head first and lying between the extended forelimbs like a high diver leaving the springboard.

The mare may show pain as the result of contractions of her uterus some hours or days before the actual act of birth, but it is only when the placenta ruptures that we recognise that delivery of the foetus is imminent. Once the placenta has ruptured and the fluid (allantoic) which it contains escapes, there is no turning back until the foetus has been expelled. During delivery the foetus remains enclosed in the second membrane or amnion, which is a shiny, thin and whitish sheet enclosing the foal and its own fluid (amniotic) (Fig 20.1). The time from the breaking of the placenta to the delivery of the foal is usually only between 15 and 45 minutes. It is always a temptation for those present to hurry this period by pulling the foal's forelegs, but this is rarely necessary or desirable under normal conditions. This is not to say that there are never any appropriate occasions for interference. Help should certainly be given, when necessary, when the foetus is lying in the wrong position (eg with one or both of the forelimbs flexed, or the head turned back). Minor adjustments of position, as when the foetus is lying a little to one side, are often accomplished by the mare getting up and down and lying on a different side, so that she herself shifts the position to the correct one.

As we have seen, the foal is lying on its back just before delivery and it may not have rotated completely as delivery proceeds. If this is the case, it may be necessary to complete the turning movement by grasping the forelegs and twisting them one over the other, to rotate the body into the upright position. If the placenta appears at the vulva lips as a thick, red membrane it may mean that the natural forces of the uterus are not causing it to rupture at the cervix as it should. In such cases, it is best to break the membrane by hand. Gentle traction on the forelimbs may also be given in cases where the mare appears to have given up efforts at expulsion, or where no progress in delivery is being made over 10 or 15 minutes.

The foal is naturally delivered with its forelimbs unevenly extended, so that the toe of one comes at about the level of the fetlock of the other. Where this difference in extension becomes more pronounced, it is sometimes helpful to ease the retarded forelimb forward but it must be remembered that the best position for delivery through the pelvis of the mother is with one elbow in advance of the other. Artificial alteration of this position can cause damage. In addition, unnatural forces such as strong traction applied to the forelimbs may easily expose the chest to damage from contact with the mother's bony pelvis during this stage of delivery. The mare gives birth lying on her side, thus normally and naturally remaining lying down for some time after she has expelled the foal. As noted, she may sometimes shift her position, apparently in an attempt to correct the position of the foal as it lies in her pelvis, so that it takes up the easiest position for delivery. However, it is only in a very few cases that the mare delivers the body of her foal while in a standing position.

It is surprising how little the pattern of behaviour of the mare has altered as a result of giving birth in a confined space and in the presence of man.

From the time that the placenta ruptures until the foal has been completely expelled, the umbilical cord and the blood vessels that it contains remain intact. In this way, throughout the whole of the birth process, the foal is receiving oxygen from the placenta and life is being maintained in the same way as it was in the uterus. When the mare has expelled her foal from the birth canal she will normally remain lying down for many minutes, often for up to half-an-hour. At first, the foal's hindlegs may remain within her vagina with the umbilical cord intact, attached at one end to the foal and at the other to the placenta within the mother's uterus. A few minutes after delivery, however, the foal becomes increasingly active and withdraws its hindlegs from the vagina, moving gradually away from the mare. This activity on the part of the foal may break the cord at a point close to the foal's belly or the cord may be broken as the mare gets to her feet. Until the foal has started to breathe and air enters the lungs for the first time, the connection between the placenta and the foal through the umbilical cord and the blood vessels that it contains is vital to the survival of the foal.

While in the mother, the air passages and small tubes of its lungs are filled with amniotic fluid. During birth, a proportion of this fluid is expelled through the nostrils as the chest is squeezed in its passage through the birth canal, so that when the foal takes its first breath in the outside world, air enters the tubes and oxygen is absorbed directly into the bloodstream. Breathing commences within seconds of expulsion from the mother, resulting in a rapid and efficient exchange of oxygen within the lungs. As the foal starts to breathe, so the blood which is in the placenta is transferred into the foal.

This means that the foal receives from the placenta what amounts to a blood transfusion of its own blood in the first minutes of life, providing that the cord remains intact. Given these facts, it can be appreciated how important it is to refrain from interfering with the cord immediately after birth. There is no justification for depriving the foal artificially of the transfusion from the placenta nor risking the possibility of prematurely cutting off its oxygen supply by early clamping or cutting of the cord. There is a natural point, an inch or so from the belly of the foal, at which the cord breaks. If mother and foal are left undisturbed and the cord remains intact in the minutes after birth, it actually becomes thinner and therefore parts

The birth of a foal

more easily at this point.

Breaking takes place naturally by the mare getting up or the foal struggling away from the mare. Unless the foal or its cord are deformed in some way, no harm can come from allowing this natural method to prevail.

Cutting the cord with scissors, as has been customary in the past, results in a stump with an unnecessary amount of dead tissue being left on the foal. In addition, cutting of the blood vessels contained in the cord is much more likely to lead to harmful bleeding from the foal than if they are torn apart in the natural manner. The sequence of cutting and haemorrhage probably accounts for another undesirable custom - the tying of the severed end of the cord with tape or ligature. This procedure adds to the risk of dead tissue being left attached to the foal, a possible focus of infection which could threaten its survival from such conditions as joint ill. The natural method of breaking leaves very little extra tissue while the blood vessels break in such a way that they automatically seal themselves so that bleeding does not occur. If it is considered necessary to break the cord artificially, the best method is to copy nature, by tugging on the cord in a direction away from the foal's belly. The stump of the cord may be treated with powder or antiseptic lotion. This practice is universally advocated and practised but whether it affords much protection against infection is open to question. If the cord is torn apart as described, the sealing mechanism of the vessels presents the most effective barrier against bacteria entering the foal's body through the umbilicus.

Once the cord is severed, the foal is independent of its mother and it only remains for her to complete the birth process by expelling the placenta. This organ is developed especially by the foal for the purpose of gaining nourishment from its mother while it lives within the uterus. Together with the membrane known as the amnion, the placenta is called the afterbirth, and it is usually expelled from the mother half to two hours after the foal. In exceptional cases, it may not separate from the mother for many hours. If it remains for more than ten, professional advice should be sought.

The sequence of events just described are those of a normal birth performed in a natural way. It must be remembered, however, that because we have 'civilised' the thoroughbred and keep it under unnatural conditions, a greater degree of variation in the behaviour of the mare is to be expected. The presence of attendants and confinement to boxes force the mare to give birth in conditions in which she must instinctively be afraid for the safety of her newborn. In these circumstances, it is not surprising, for instance, to find mares who get to their feet immediately they have expelled their foal or they may even give birth while in the standing position. If, the position of the foal is seen to be normal and the birth process proceeding at a reasonable speed and in a satisfactory manner, the less intrusion on the mare's privacy at this particular time, the more likely events will follow a natural sequence.

It is sometimes assumed that a mare may tread on her foal when standing up if it is not pulled in front of her immediately it is delivered. However, it is most unlikely that she will injure her offspring in this manner unless she is startled by some unexpected event such as the entrance of men into her box. Even on such occasions, it is very exceptional that she will hurt her foal, as the instinct to avoid treading on the newborn is extremely well-developed in nearly all mares.

In deciding whether or not a newborn foal is normal and healthy, it is important to know something of the history of the birth through which it has just passed. For this reason, note should be made of certain landmarks during each and every birth, recording them in a book or on a special form in case needed later. The main points, with some values as a basis for a normal range in brackets, are:

(1) The number of days of pregnancy (320-350 days)

(2) The number of minutes between the rupture of the placenta (breaking of the water) and complete delivery, ie the expulsion of the foal's body and hips from the mother (10-45 mins)

(3) The time between complete delivery and the breaking of the cord (1-30 mins)

(4) The time taken for the foal to get to its feet and to take its first suck from the mother (15-90 mins)

(5) The time at which the afterbirth is finally expelled from the mother (15 mins - 4 hours), together with any comments as to any unusual feature seen on its surface.

Such information can be of vital importance to a vet who has been called to a sick foal in the first few days of life.

The birth of a foal

21: The newborn foal

For 11 months, while the foal develops within the mother's uterus completely surrounded by the placenta, it is, to a very large extent, protected from contact with infectious agents such as bacteria and viruses. It is only rarely that infections from the mother cross the placental barrier and affect the developing foal. A notable exception is the herpes (rhinopneumonitis) virus, which normally affects the respiratory system of the mare, passes into the foetus and causes abortion.

At the end of the 11 months, the foal is born and it then leaves the protective surroundings of the uterus for the rigours of the outside world. The young foal is surprisingly ill-equipped to meet the challenge of the new environment and the abounding fungi, bacteria and virus which inhabit it. While the foal is in the uterus none of the protective antibodies which are the basis of resistance pass from the mother, nor is the foal capable of producing its own antibodies for several weeks, if not months. The mare does, in fact, provide for the protection of the foal after birth by supplying it with a high concentration of her own antibodies in the colostrum, or first milk of her udder. When the newborn foal takes this milk into its stomach, it absorbs the vital antibodies into its own bloodstream.

After about 12 to 24 hours the ability of the foal to absorb antibodies through the lining of the stomach comes to an end. For the rest of its life, the giving of antibodies by mouth is therefore no longer a practical method of providing immunity. Other methods, such as hypodermic injections, have to be used. The transfer of the mother's antibodies to her offspring through the colostrum gives the final protection for a limited number of weeks by which time, however, the foal should have developed a capacity for producing its own antibodies.

The exact type of antibodies which the mother possesses and which she therefore passes to the foal, are governed by the challenge of the infectious agents in her immediate surroundings and the response that this challenge has evoked in her bloodstream. For instance, a mare infected with the influenza cough virus during the last month or so of pregnancy will probably possess a high level of antibodies against this virus and will pass the same antibodies to her foal after it is born, through the colostrum. The foal will then be protected for several weeks against the same influenza virus. However, if the mother has never been in contact with the virus, she will possess none of these antibodies and neither will her newborn foal.

Since the antibodies for one infective agent will not protect for another, keeping a pregnant mare on one stud and moving her shortly before she foals, may deprive her offspring of protection from some of the infective agents of the environment into which it is born. The main challenge to the resistance of the newborn foal comes from the bacteria which abound in the surroundings of the box, especially from faeces-contaminated bedding and, to a lesser extent, from the organisms in the soil and pasture of the paddocks.

The main routes of entry of bacteria into the foal's body are through the mouth, airways or umbilicus, where the navel or umbilical cord has so recently been ruptured (hence the term 'navel ill' applied to certain types of infection seen in the newborn). In umbilical infections, an abscess forms and may be seen on occasions as a swelling outside the umbilicus, though more commonly it is to be found only at post-mortem just inside the abdomen, giving no evidence externally. An abscess in this position may result, after a matter of days or even weeks, in the symptoms of lockjaw or tetanus, but another condition which is often thought to follow infection of the navel is that of 'joint ill'. The terms joint ill and navel ill usually refer to the same condition. The bacteria gain entrance to one or more of the joints, setting up an arthritis within the joint so that the animal goes lame and may run a high temperature. The severity of symptoms in joint ill depends on the amount of destruction the infection causes within the joint. If the cartilage which lines the joint surface becomes eroded and ulcerated and, if the bone adjacent to the joint becomes diseased, the outlook will be very serious. In some cases, the infection merely results in an increased amount of fluid in the joint. This subsides with treatment, although it may be necessary to continue treatment over a number of weeks before the condition finally settles. In other cases, pus forms within the joint and there is much destruction of the adjacent structures forming the joint.

Remarkable progress in the treatment of joint ill has been made in recent years, and the outlook for affected individuals is now much better than it was, say, a decade ago. Not only has an ever-widening range of antibiotics and anti-inflammatory drugs, such as corticosteroids and pain-relievers been added to the veterinary surgeon's armoury, but the technique of introducing such drugs directly into the joint has revolutionised the treatment of joint ill. There is a natural barrier between the bloodstream and the joints which normally protects them from infection but, once this has been breached, and infection has entered the joint, the self-same barrier appears to shelter the infective agents against antibiotics given by mouth or by intra-muscular injection. If introduced directly into the joint, however, such drugs are very much more effective and dramatic results often follow. Although a foal may apparently completely recover from joint ill, the effect may still be seen when it has grown into a racehorse. At this time, when the pressure of training is applied, lameness may again occur from the damage originally caused to the joint.

Bacteria, virus or fungus can enter the body of a developing foal before it is born and, in this case, they may already have become established at the time of birth. In such cases, the protective mechanism or antibody umbrella, which shields the newborn foal may be developed too late to give protection so that very early in life it may succumb to septicaemia or infection of one of the major organs of the body. The kidney is very often affected by these early pre-natal infections. A weak foal, which has difficulty in getting up in the first 12 hours of life, then appears to make some progress towards the end of the first day only to become progressively weaker until it eventually dies, is a typical example of one affected in this way. Bacteria such as E coli and BVE (bacterium viscosum equi) are frequent causes of this early infectious disease which overwhelms the normal protective mechanism of the newborn foal.

It is thought that some of these early diseases are the result of infection being present or introduced as far back as the time when the mare was covered by the stallion. Because the fight against bacteria has been so successfully waged by the use of antibiotics, measures to prevent the introduction of infectious diseases which were so essential in pre-antibiotic days are now often forgotten. The wheel may, however, be turning full circle as an increasing number of drug-resistant bacteria are being encountered in foals, as in the young of other species. Attention to hygiene and application of the general principles of disease prevention are therefore again becoming increasingly important.

The greater the resistance of the newborn foal, the higher its chances of survival, and in the management of pregnant mares this fact must not be overlooked. It is during the last two months of pregnancy that the immunity of the newborn foal is prepared and in the first 12 hours of life that it is normally transferred. In order to withstand the challenge of its new surroundings, the foal must be born in a mature condition. What is meant by 'maturity', or the 'mature state', when applied in this context?

The use of two or more words to describe the same condition is bound to lead to confusion. The terms prematurity and immaturity as applied to the newly-born foal clearly illustrate the potential for confusion. To be mature is to be completely or fully-developed but, with regard to the body, the term must always be qualified by stating the purposes for which maturity is required. For instance, we do not expect an animal to be sexually mature at birth, nor that the bones be in a state of full development before the animal is three or four years old. Maturity is achieved in different organs at different times of life.

A state of maturity in the newborn can be taken as meaning that the organs have reached a sufficient level of development to sustain life and meet the requirements of the body under average conditions. Failure of any one of the organs vital to survival means that the foal is at risk immediately it is born. This lack of maturity is generally defined as 'immaturity'. The effects of immaturity, once the foal is born, will be a matter of degree and also depend on circumstances outside the body (ie the severity of the challenge of the surroundings). In simple terms, a foal born with a slight degree of immaturity may be able to overcome the difficulties of adjustment that this will impose, providing such conditions as temperature and so on under which it is born are not too severe. Artificial ways of raising the foal's temperature, feeding it, and aiding it in other ways, become necessary, therefore, for a slightly immature foal's survival. The greater the degree of immaturity, however, the less likely that successful adaptation will occur whatever artificial aids are applied. In fact, when a foal is born with extreme immaturity, it cannot possibly survive outside the uterus and it is said to be non-viable. Such extreme cases are seen when a mare aborts or delivers her foal several weeks before the normally appointed time.

What is meant by the term 'degree of immaturity'? From the time of conception, the various organs of the body of the foetus start to develop and grow. Each organ has a different rate of development and, as has been said, the maturity of the body as a whole depends on the organs necessary for survival having reached a sufficient level of development to meet the requirements of the body at any particular time. One of the most important organs for survival after birth are the lungs. Whereas the foetus has little or no need of the lungs because it is receiving oxygen from its mother, once this connection has been severed immediately after birth, survival depends on the efficient functioning of the lungs to supply the demands of the body for oxygen.

By following the development of the lungs through foetal life it becomes apparent that they cannot possibly function efficiently before a certain stage has been reached. In the equine foetus, this stage is probably reached at about ten months of pregnancy. Before that time, the cells lining the air sacs are not sufficiently developed to allow the passage of gases between the air and the bloodstream to occur normally. In addition, a chemical substance which must be present in the air sacs to allow the lungs to expand properly does not appear until the last four weeks or so of pregnancy. Although the lungs have been used as an example, the same process of development applies to other organs such as the kidneys, brain, liver and so on. Although individual organs have been cited, it is usual to speak of total effects in terms of the whole animal. A foal is therefore said to have been born immature, not that it has been born with immature lungs.

Prefixes besides 'im-' given to the term 'maturity' also cause confusion. The most frequent is 'prematurity'. This term means exactly the same as immaturity. It is usually used with a definite inference that the lack of maturity arises from the fact that the foetus has not been kept for sufficient time within the uterus to attain the necessary state of development or maturity at birth. In other words, the newborn is immature because it is born too soon.

In the horse it is known that the normal length of pregnancy is between 320 and 350 days, with an average of about 335. It is also known that a foal born well before the average time, say four or five weeks, has very little chance of surviving, because it will be much too immature. If it is born earlier than this, to a pregnancy less than 300 days, it will certainly not survive. It is then customary to call the birth an abortion.

The term 'post mature' might be considered to be the opposite of 'premature', indicating that the pregnancy has gone over the normal length of time. For a mare to carry her foal a year is certainly not unknown, and cases of even longer duration have been recorded. One might expect that the extra time spent in the uterus would result in the birth of a foal very much larger than the average. However, it is found that quite the opposite occurs, the foal being small and sometimes with the clinical appearances of being immature. It might be argued that the foetus has been retained for the extra time in an attempt to establish full development or maturity.

The newborn foal

Most of the terms that have been mentioned have been borrowed from medicine.

In the horse-breeding industry, the term premature is used for a sick foal which cannot adjust to the environment but which may have been born at any time before the normal length of pregnancy, or even those that are carried well beyond this time. It would be more logical and would reduce confusion to use the term immaturity and drop the term prematurity.

The term 'stillborn' is used when a foal is born in a dead or dying condition to a pregnancy of normal length. It implies that the foal has not breathed, although it may gasp for a few seconds after it has been expelled.

Diseases of the newborn foal are generally those illnesses that affect the foal during the first week or so of life. The newborn foal, biologically speaking, is the 11 month old foetus which has just passed through the experience of the birth process - an event lasting only an hour, but which poses a potential hazard in the transition between foetal life and that outside the uterus. The health of the newborn depends firstly on the state of health of the foetus at the end of pregnancy and then on its smooth and unharmed passage through the birth canal. The individual which has been ill as a foetus or which has suffered damage during the birth process is seen as a sick foal in the days following birth. Thus, many of the diseases of the newborn foal originate at a time when they are beyond observation or diagnosis. A substantial proportion of all foals sick in the first week of life suffer from foetal illness or become ill through experiences at birth. Describing the various conditions of this large group of diseases affecting the newborn are such terms as 'prematures', 'immatures', 'barkers', 'wanderers', 'dummies', 'weak foals' and so on. There is a certain amount of confusion in the use of these terms as they are often employed to describe conditions arising from dissimilar causes but which have apparently similar symptoms. One characteristic they have in common is that they refer to a sick foal suffering, not from an infectious agent (bacteria, viruses, etc), but from the failure of the individual to adapt itself to its new environment outside the uterus. This group of illnesses might be defined as 'diseases of failure to adapt or adjust to an independent existence'.

Before explaining these terms individually, it is appropriate to take a brief look at the problems which affect the newborn and which have to be overcome if it is successfully to establish itself as a new individual in the world.

The first and most vital problem for the foal is the need to obtain oxygen from the air within minutes of emergence from the uterus, so that the level of this gas in the blood is adequate for its needs. In foetal life and during birth, the oxygen content is maintained because the blood collects the gas from the mother as it passes through the placenta via the umbilical cord. If the amount of oxygen in the blood falls below a minimum level, even for a few minutes, there may be dramatic and deleterious effects on certain tissues of the body, especially the brain, lungs and kidneys. These harmful effects may not be fatal but may result in the newborn being weakened in such a way that the ability to adjust or adapt will be markedly reduced.

The first breath

Breathing is living and the first breath marks the beginning of life in the world and signals the end the end of foetal life. The replacement of the placenta by the lungs as the organ responsible for gaseous exchange requires a radical re-routing of the blood within the body. In the hours after birth, these radical changes of the circulation are taking place within the body of the foal.

Breathing, once established, supplies the oxygen necessary to sustain the heroic muscular exertions required to raise the foal to its feet within an hour or two of birth. During foetal life, the weight of the foal has been supported by the fluid surrounding it and by the organs of the mother. Now, for the first time, it feels the pull of gravity, and its muscles are expected to act in a quite unaccustomed manner. Anyone who has experienced a prolonged sojourn in bed will appreciate the difficulties of standing for the first time! Small wonder that enormously increased requirements of energy are needed by the foal in the first three hours of life. Fortunately, the lungs are relatively very much more efficient than the placenta as a means of gaseous exchange, so the new demands for oxygen are easily met.

A dramatic fall in temperature is another difference that has to be faced by the newborn in its fresh surroundings. The swimming pool of its foetal life, thermostatically controlled by the mother at about 100°F (38°C), is exchanged for an air temperature some 50°-60°F (10°-16°C) less.

At birth the foal must also face the problem of getting rid of its own waste material through the kidneys and the gut. Both systems have now to function in a somewhat different manner from the way in which they were behaving in the foetus. This is especially true of the gut, which for the first time has to accept food in the form of milk. Before the milk can pass through the length of the gut, the foal has to evacuate its meconium. This is the dung which has been stored during foetal life within the large bowel (colon, caecum and rectum). The foal very rarely passes dung while it is in the uterus and it is quite abnormal for it to do so. It can be appreciated, therefore, that immediately after birth the muscles of the bowel wall have to act in a somewhat different way than previously. The difficulties that some foals experience during the first three days of life in the passing of the first dung, or meconium, is well recognised by stud grooms.

These are just a few of the vital problems which have to be overcome by the foal during the first few days after birth. However, the reader should not gain the impression that the majority of newly-born do not accomplish the process of adjustment smoothly and without trouble.

But in an appreciation of their problems lies the foundation for a style of management likely to give the greatest help to the foal, from the earliest days of pregnancy, through birth and the period of adaptation.

When dealing with a sick foal, that which has begun badly may have to be remedied by artificial means unless they are to become worse and the foal is to

succumb to the challenge of its environment. For instance, a foal born with inadequate reserves of food within its body or damaged in some way by the birth process may require artificial aids such as feeding by stomach tube or being kept warm by raising the temperature of the surroundings. On the other hand, a foal born in a quite normal and healthy state will probably withstand great insults to its body in the form of low temperatures, exposure to infection, and even a prolonged birth process, without any apparent untoward effects.

Barkers, wanderers and dummies

Terms such as 'barkers', 'dummies', 'wanderers' and 'prematures' usually refer to prominent symptoms seen when the normal behaviour pattern is destroyed. By 'behaviour pattern' is meant the normal reactions of a foal to its surroundings. We therefore include in the term the fact that the foal starts to breathe within a few seconds of birth and then immediately attempts to get to its feet, that it will achieve a standing position within an hour or so of birth, and that once on its feet it will seek out its mother's udder and take milk from her.

From that point the foal will get up and down on its own and feed at regular intervals, gaining an ever-increasing awareness of its surroundings. Such awareness includes an attachment towards its mother, which it recognises as the source of its nourishment, and a sense of fear of other factors in its world such as the presence of men in the box.

The first symptoms of a failure to adapt are seen within 24 hours of birth, *ie* during the period when there is the greatest necessity for adjustment between foetal and newborn life. As might be expected from a highly complex mechanism such as the body, the symptoms that appear can take a variety of forms, ranging from those that are mild and hardly noticeable to those that are severe and dramatic. In some cases, therefore, no more than vague symptoms may be seen. Perhaps the foal will take longer than usual to rise to its feet for the first time or to suck. Maybe the effects on behaviour will be so slight that an experienced onlooker may know instinctively that it is abnormal without being able to pinpoint the problems.

At the other end of the scale, a foal may have convulsions - jerky movements of the body and limbs, with champing jaws, giving way to violent uncoordinated movements with the foal lying on one side making frantic efforts as if to gallop or rise to its feet. The body temperature is likely to rise and profuse sweating occur during such excessive activity. Between episodes of convulsions the foal is likely to go into periods of deep coma. If it is able to stand, it may wander round the box aimlessly, perhaps bumping into the walls or, alternatively, standing dummy-like showing no interest in its surroundings. The foal usually loses its ability to recognise its mother or to feed itself by sucking in this type of illness - always so in severe cases.

There are wide variations between different individuals in the number of such symptoms which may actually appear. On the one hand, there are foals that have convulsions, coma and aimless wandering while others may have no convulsions but only the loss of ability to suck and recognise the mare.

The term 'barker' has been given to foals that have convulsions because some of them will emit a noise like a dog barking while they are suffering from them. The labels 'wanderer' and 'dummy' are given to other cases where convulsions are absent and the less severe symptoms predominate.

A proportion of foals that have difficulty in adapting to their life outside the uterus die, but a large number recover and grow up to perform creditably on the racecourse. The time taken to recover or adapt fully may take from a day to a week or more. In fact, complete restoration of a normal behaviour pattern, including the ability to suck from the mother, may not be restored in some cases for several weeks.

Failure to adapt

There may be a number of different causes for the failure of the newborn to adjust to the environment, while many of the symptoms that result may be the same.

One obvious and well-known cause is a lack of oxygen which damages nerve cells and blood vessels in many parts of the body. Certain minimal levels of oxygen are required in the bloodstream at all times. It is true that in the foetal state and during birth, when there is little or no muscular activity, the requirements will be less than after birth. There are occasions, nevertheless, when even those low requirements cannot be met in full because of a separation of the placenta from its close apposition with the uterus, or because of other factors, such as an interference with the circulation in the umbilical cord before the lungs have become expanded and are capable of supplying the necessary gaseous exchange between the air and the bloodstream.

Even after birth when the foal has become detached from the cord, the lungs may fail to expand properly or perform their function efficiently. In all such cases, the lack of oxygen may be only temporary and not sufficiently extreme to kill the animal. Nevertheless, nerve cells and blood vessels in various parts of the body may be damaged and the consequent effects will seriously endanger the capacity of the animal to adjust and overcome the problems presented by its new environment.

'Anoxia' or 'hypoxia', as this lack of oxygen is often called, may trigger a chain reaction by interfering with or damaging one organ which, in turn, may affect many others. For instance, lack of oxygen may destroy certain substances in the lung which are vital to the normal expansion in the first minutes or hours of life, and so lead to insufficient expansion and inefficiency in the methods of gaseous exchange. The consequence will be an additional lack of oxygen and an upset will be caused in the chemical composition of the blood. The kidneys and circulation will, in turn, become disturbed. It is hardly surprising, therefore, that the effects of such a chain

The newborn foal

reaction will be reflected in a variety of symptoms in a foal so affected.

Another and more direct way in which the circulation can become disturbed is as a result of pressure on the heart during birth. The heart lies in the chest, very close to the surface, and is protected only by the thin ribs of the chest wall. It is quite possible for the heart muscle to be bruised during birth or, in extreme cases, when the ribs become broken, the fractured ends may even gouge into the sides of the heart, causing death.

These, then, are just some of the factors that can interfere with normal adjustment of the foal during the first few days of life. Treatment in these cases consists largely of good nursing and restoring the balance between the attempts of the body to survive against the challenge of the environment. Frequent feeding through a stomach tube supplies energy and nourishment during the time that the foal is unable to suck. Providing more air warmth helps to maintain the body temperature when the regulating mechanism of the body is impaired due to the inactivity of coma and of the 'dummy' state.

If a foal is unable to stand, the presence of a man in the box to support it when it tries to get to its feet can minimise the amount of energy required by the foal when it tries to exert itself. At the same time, it is necessary to prevent the foal from hitting its head on the ground or rubbing its eyes on the straw while it is incapable of getting up on its own. Many a foal's life has been saved by a conscientious studsman nursing it on the ground with its head on his lap. A constant watch is often kept in this manner through 24 hours of the day.

The effort required by studs during the foaling season, a time of maximum activity, in the nursing of sick foals, is not always realised or appreciated by owners. Sedatives and other drugs may help, but good nursing makes all the difference.

Jaundiced foals

Most people have heard of rhesus ('yellow') babies and many horse breeders have had the misfortune to breed a foal which suddenly becomes jaundiced ('yellow') soon after birth. Only babies and newborn foals suffer from the disease. There are various minor differences in the way each is involved, but the two deep basic causes are similar.

Firstly, there must be an important inherited difference between the mother's and her offspring's type of red blood corpuscles. Secondly, at some time during pregnancy, the unborn foal's (or baby's) corpuscles must leak into its mother's circulation.

A foal inherits either its father's or its mother's type of corpuscles. There is about an equal chance of them being either type. Whichever it turns out to be, the tiny embryo quickly commences to manufacture all its own blood of the particular inherited type. It continues to do this for the rest of its life, both inside the mother and after it is born. While it is in the womb, a foal's blood comes into very close contact with its mother's, but there should never be any mixing. The two blood

circulations are separated by a thin barrier and dissolved food material, oxygen and waste products are freely exchanged across it. However, the barrier is impervious to red blood corpuscles, unless damaged in some way. Minute defects or breaches somewhere in the barrier between mother's and foal's circulation are not uncommon and often lead to some abnormal change of corpuscles.

If the foal's corpuscles are one of several types (inherited from the sire), which are very different from its dam's, they react in her just like any foreign material. She soon produces powerful antibodies in her blood to destroy the alien matter. That is to say, she produces substances which are very efficient in destroying the red corpuscles of her own foal although, of course, these antibodies are primarily intended to eliminate something which has got into her own blood by accident from the foal in the womb. When this happens the antibodies may increase enormously in quantity during the last few weeks of pregnancy.

When the mare commences to produce her first milk (or colostrum) the concentration of antibodies during the first few days becomes far greater even than it is in blood. For about 36 hours or a little longer after its birth, a sucking foal can freely absorb antibodies through its gut into the bloodstream. This is the real danger period. Soon afterwards, this power of absorption is lost, so that the 'dangerous' milk may be sucked without risk. There are methods by which a laboratory can predict with reasonable certainty whether a foal is likely to become jaundiced if allowed to take its mother's colostrum. In such a case, it is sufficient to prevent it sucking during the first two days in order to eliminate entirely the possibility of the disease. This is done by muzzling the foal, which may be fed during the period by milk from a 'safe' mare. In infants the destructive substances pass into the baby while it is in the womb. In foals, they come only via the first milk. However, colostrum contains some most important protective substances which a foal can ill afford to be without. Deliberately depriving it of the milk to prevent jaundice incurs a great risk of the foal developing a serious infection.

There is a similar problem when a mare runs milk for some days before its foal is born - the colostrum is lost. The risk of infection can be taken care of to some extent by administering antibiotics for a few days. But there is no complete substitute for colostrum. Foals which are muzzled to prevent them sucking during the first 48 hours all too frequently fall victims to a septicaemia. Colostrum from other mares given to muzzled foals would help to prevent this but, in practice, it is very difficult to arrange supplies.

Jaundiced (sometimes called haemolytic) foals are not really common but, despite the best of treatment, the mortality rate among them is high and the loss of an otherwise excellent foal is a severe blow to a breeder and is extremely disappointing. Prevention of the disease is by no means easy. It is very rare in first foals. So the first case from a mare comes as a complete surprise. Once a mare has had one such foal there is a much increased likelihood of her having another at a future time. Some steps can be taken to cope with the possibility. Blood samples

from the mare should be examined late in pregnancy. Ideally, three, taken at weekly intervals before the expected birth, should be tested. It is only during the last month that most mares start to react very clearly. Sometimes only a test taken during the final ten days of pregnancy reveals the extent of the danger. By testing at intervals during the eleventh month it can be judged how much destructive antibody is building up in the mother's blood for later transfer to the milk (together with the useful protective substances).

If there is a continuous rise, the foal must not be allowed to suck from her for two days. If it does, the damaging antibodies will enter the bloodstream and proceed to destroy a substantial proportion of the foal's red corpuscles. This leads to very severe jaundice and anaemia and sometimes to the passing of red urine. The red blood corpuscles carry all the oxygen around the body and if they are insufficient the animal soon becomes depleted of this vital gas and shows corresponding symptoms. It yawns repeatedly and becomes extremely lethargic. It rests a great deal and, if disturbed, quickly gets out of breath. Because of the destruction of its red corpuscles and some subsequent reactions, the mouth and eye membranes become a bright canary yellow colour.

There are some other diseases of newborn foals where slight jaundice appears, but none so striking as in this particular condition. The disease comes on with dramatic suddenness, soon after the first suck in most instances, and certainly within the first 36 hours. The first thing the vet requires is a blood sample, which is examined to see how severe the blood destruction has been. Sometimes it may not be bad enough to warrant giving the foal a transfusion. If so, the animal is merely watched carefully for any deterioration, and this is gauged by further blood examinations and a study of its general condition.

Many affected foals require a transfusion of cells, of a type which the harmful antibody from the mother's milk does not destroy. This and the transfusion process is undertaken by the attending vet in collaboration with an appropriate laboratory. In numerous cases, the effects of a transfusion lead to spectacular improvement and recovery. It may be necessary to repeat the procedure several times. Nevertheless, it should be noted that here we are dealing with an acute disease with a potentially high death rate. Many foals die.

Those who have lost a foal with haemolytic jaundice often ask whether it is possible to eliminate the risk subsequently by testing the blood of the proposed stallion against the mare's. Theoretically this would minimise the risks, but there is only the remotest chance that stallion owners would ever permit such a procedure, even in isolated cases. There is even less possibility that wholesale testing of stallion blood against all visiting mares could ever be contemplated. In fact, there is as little possibility of that (although for entirely different reasons) as expecting that humans might not marry on account of some differences in their blood types likely to lead to jaundiced babies.

Diarrhoea

Diarrhoea in foals is an all too common condition on thoroughbred studs. It causes much concern to stud grooms and vets alike. When a foal has diarrhoea it is often said to be 'purging', 'scouring', 'wet' or 'damp'. All these terms are descriptive of the condition of the dung or faeces but in fact diarrhoea is only a symptom. Even the nature of the diarrhoea (*ie* whether the faeces are thick and pasty, bloodstained or like water) tells us very little of the causes, of which there are many.

One of the commonest forms of diarrhoea is seen in foals at the time when the mare is 'in season'. At this time, chemical substances are found in the milk which irritate the bowel wall and cause the foal to have loose dungs for several days. This type of scour is not serious and usually stops when the mare goes out of season.

It is often very difficult or impossible, in our present state of knowledge, to diagnose with certainty the cause of diarrhoea in any particular foal or group of foals. It is known, however, that bacteria are often associated with the condition. Bacteria are very small organisms which can be seen only under the microscope. They have certain characteristics by which laboratory workers can easily classify them into groups and families. One of the commonest bacteria associated with diarrhoea in young animals is one known as *Escherichia coli*. Strains of this germ are normally found in the bowel contents but for different reasons they may become 'hotted-up' and so cause an infectious type of diarrhoea. Another type of bacteria that can cause diarrhoea in foals belongs to a group known as salmonella. Unlike *E coli*, this bacterium is not normally present in the bowel and, when it is, is almost certain to cause very severe illness. In the salmonella group are also found the germs which cause food poisoning and dysentery in humans. There are many other bacteria which may possibly play a part in diarrhoea in foals, and future research may come to incriminate with greater certainty.

Certain viruses cause diarrhoea. The most common is rotavirus, so named because of its wheel-like shape. Other forms of rotavirus cause diarrhoea and inflammation of the bowel in children, calves, piglets, lambs and other species. However, each species tends to have its own specific rotavirus that does not infect others. Rotavirus is very resistant and exists on paddocks or in buildings over many months. Foals obtain resistance through the mare's milk. Outbreaks of diarrhoea occur only when the resistance of the individual is diminished by stress or when the antibody content of the mare's milk is low and the amount of rotavirus in the environment is high.

Salmonella infection is fortunately a rare occurrence in thoroughbreds but, if one foal becomes infected, the disease usually spreads quite rapidly to other foals on the premises and there may be several deaths as a result. The cause of this kind of diarrhoea can be fairly easily established by taking swabs from the rectum and growing the organism in the laboratory.

It is often difficult to make a definite diagnosis of other causes of diarrhoea. The

The newborn foal

foal's faeces may be tested for rotavirus and, if found to be positive, this is likely to be the cause although studies have shown that rotavirus may be recovered from foals not suffering from diarrhoea and, conversely, not found in some individuals suffering diarrhoea, despite the presence of the virus in other foals. In these circumstances, it may be assumed that the affected individuals are nevertheless infected with the virus. Very often several foals are affected on one stud at the same time, which gives the appearance that the condition is infectious, spreading from one animal to another.

However, it may well be that certain factors in the foals' environment may make them particularly liable to develop diarrhoea. Such factors are often referred to as predisposing factors. With regard to diarrhoea in foals, there are many different predisposing causes which have to be considered, but probably one of the most important is a sudden lowering of the ambient air temperature leading to body cooling. Draughts are especially likely to lead to such conditions and the type of buildings commonly found on studs in this country, which were often built many years ago, are particularly liable to draughts and sudden marked changes in the air temperature over the 24 hours of a day. Another circumstance in which there may be considerable cooling of the foal's body, is when the young foal gets wet and is then perhaps brought into a draughty box. At the same time, while the foal is confined to a box, it is in surroundings where bacteria, especially E coli, are prevalent.

Rapidly growing grass, such as is found during a rainy spell after dry conditions, may also predispose a foal to diarrhoea. In this case it is often referred to as a 'grass scour'. At about four weeks of age, the foal starts to take increasing amounts of dry matter, such as hay, oats and even straw. These substances may at first cause irritation of the bowel and result in diarrhoea. This is said to be a nutritional diarrhoea, but it may become complicated by any of the common causes listed above.

Diarrhoea may occur in foals any time from birth onwards. There is every degree of severity, ranging from the foal which is merely 'damp' for a few hours to those that pass what appears to be practically pure water. The foal may be so sick that it stops sucking from the mare. Its coat will stand on end, there may be signs of pain and the tongue may become coated. The eyes may sink into the orbits and there can be a rapid loss of body condition with wasting of the muscles. These latter symptoms are due to the great loss of fluid that occurs if the diarrhoea is profuse. Not only is water lost from the body but, with it, vital substances known as electrolytes (such as the minerals sodium and potassium, and also bicarbonate). Electrolytes are necessary for maintaining the balance required for the proper functioning of individual cells. If a foal loses large quantities it may die as a direct result.

To treat such a case, vets therefore give fluid containing the same electrolytes by mouth or as a transfusion into the bloodstream, in order to replace the loss. This is especially important if the foal has gone 'off suck' and is taking in no fluid on its own account. Affected foals will often drink large quantities of water and they should not be stopped from doing so unless the fluid is being replaced in another way. They will almost certainly die of dehydration if they are losing fluid which is not being replaced.

It is often thought that scouring in foals is caused by drinking water in excess. Although this actually may be the case, especially if a foal has been 'gorging' its salt lick, it is much more probable that the foals drink because they have lost water in the diarrhoea.

As well as replacing the fluid and lost electrolytes, vets give antibiotics by mouth and by injection in order to kill any offending bacteria in the bowel.

Prevention of scouring is made difficult by the fact that it is not always possible to diagnose the exact cause and because there are many predisposing factors which may have to be taken into account. In the first two months of life, foals have reserves which are much less than those found in older foals. Diarrhoea in younger foals is more likely to be serious, or even fatal, than in the older group. For this reason, foals are often given antibiotics during the first few days of life, as is the practice in the calf-rearing industry where a similar problem arises.

It is interesting that whenever diarrhoeas are found on one stud in thoroughbred foals, the condition will probably be found at the same time on very many other studs in different parts of the country. This suggests that the changeable weather or the state of growth of the pasture, including the weeds it contains, may play some part.

Epidemics of diarrhoea are known in most species of animals where they are housed in artificial conditions. Epidemic diarrhoea among babies is also experienced in hospitals.

The effect on the thoroughbred breeding industry is probably not severe in terms of financial loss, although some potentially valuable animals can die or their growth be retarded if the illness is severe. The great majority of foals that suffer from diarrhoea, however, eventually recover without any ill effect.

22: Orphan foals

Between January and May, we often hear appeals (through the press and even on television) for a foster mother. There are a number of reasons why a foal cannot be reared by its natural mother. One of the main ones, of course, is that the mare dies while giving birth or very shortly afterwards. It is on record that a foal was saved, and survived, when the mare died just before going into labour. A knife was used speedily and the foal was delivered through the flank of the dead mother.

The most common cause of sudden death of a mare during birth is from internal haemorrhage. The vessel that usually ruptures is the artery which supplies blood to the uterus. The uterus at the time of birth contains a foal weighing perhaps 100-120lb (approximately 50kg) together with the membranes and fluid which surround it. The whole uterus is supported by a thin sheet called the broad ligament. The main artery carrying blood to the uterus runs in this suspending membrane. During birth there are tremendous strains exerted on these structures and it is not surprising that, from time to time, the artery breaks. If it does, the bleeding may occur directly into the abdominal cavity and the animal literally bleeds to death within a few minutes. This may occur at any time during or shortly after birth. It is possible for this artery to break but for the blood to become contained within the broad ligament itself and not burst into the abdominal cavity. In this case, although a great deal of blood may be lost to the circulation, there will not be a fatal result.

There are other disasters which may occur during birth which end in death or destruction of the mare. These include tearing of the uterus so that the bowel passes through the vagina to the exterior, and prolapse or eversion of the uterus so that it turns inside out and comes through the vagina to the outside. There may also be coincidental happenings resulting in death through such conditions as colic or infection.

The relationship of the mother to the offspring is mainly one of supplying food in the form of milk. The foal, until it is about four months old, depends very largely upon milk for its nourishment. Although from about two weeks onwards, it may take an increasing amount of solid food in the form of hay, oats or grass, it nevertheless requires the easily digestible and nutritious contents of milk. The regular intake of the fluid which milk supplies is of the utmost importance to the body if dehydration is to be prevented. The latter is seen in loss of weight and an unthrifty condition.

From the udder of the mare, the foal is able to suck milk whenever it feels like it, perhaps every twenty minutes or so. In each 24 hours it may be supplied with as much as three gallons of milk from the mare. Foals can be reared by bottle but it is most unlikely that natural conditions can be entirely simulated. Bottle-fed foals may do well, but this method of rearing usually leaves its mark upon their bodies. It sometimes happens that after a mare has foaled, there is very little milk in the mammary glands. The mare may become dry if she is ill or if the foal is prevented from sucking through illness for several days. Alternatively, a mare may not accept the foal and allow it to suck. In rare cases, she will even attack the foal so that they have to be separated. In all such cases it is necessary to find alternative methods of rearing. By far the most satisfactory is to get another mare to accept the foal, so that she will rear it as her own.

Those who work on studs expect a foal normally to rise to its feet within an hour, at the most two, of birth. By the time it is three hours old, it will generally have found its way to its mother and be sucking from the udder. The mother also welcomes the foal, licking it, calling to it, and mothering it. But there are minor exceptions to this pattern. Some mares, especially when they have their first foal, are very reluctant when the foal makes its first attempt to suck. Some foals have less sense than others, in the first few hours, of where to find the food. These behaviour patterns of mare and foal are examples of innate reflexes and appear in the horse immediately it is born and do not have to be learned.

How a mare recognises a foal as being her own is not known, but once she has smelt it or licked it, she will develop a mothering instinct specifically for that foal. It has been suggested in relation to other species that it is the fluid which surrounds the foal at birth, known as the amniotic fluid, which triggers maternal behaviour. The mare will not normally tolerate a foal other than her own feeding from her. A foal, however, is not nearly as choosy. If the sucking reflex and the desire to suck are present, and it is hungry, it will usually take food from any mare if allowed to do so.

When a foster mother is found, it is necessary to persuade her that the orphan foal is her own. There is a varying response by individual mares to efforts to deceive them, to enable the orphan foal to be accepted. It is necessary that the foster mother should recently have lost her own foal, preferably near to the time of birth. If too much time has elapsed between the loss of her own foal and the introduction of the orphan foal, the udder will have dried up and there will be no milk available. The longer from birth, the more attached is the foster mother to her own foal and it is less likely that she will accept a stranger. The temperament of the mare and the strength of her maternal instincts are equally important.

Many ruses are used by vets and stud grooms when attempting to put an orphan foal on a foster mother. These must vary according to circumstances. If a mare is exposed to a foal that sucks regularly from its udder, she will readily become attached to it. If, therefore, measures are taken to prevent her from kicking the foal, this method may succeed. Some studfarms have a partition arranged so that the mare is placed on one side and the foal on the other. The foal is thus able to suck from the mare through a conveniently placed opening at the level of her udder. Another measure aimed at preventing the foal from being kicked is to administer tranquillisers. Care must be taken to ensure that the mare does not come round from the tranquiliser unexpectedly and kick the foal.

Here are some other approaches to the problem of fostering. If a mare had a dead foal (or one that died in the first few weeks of life) and is to become a foster mother, it is best to leave the carcass of her foal in the box until the orphan foal has arrived at the stud. The potential foster mother is then taken from the box, the carcass removed and the orphan foal put inside. The foal may be rubbed with the amnion of the foster mother's foal, if this is available, or some strong smelling ointment rubbed on the mare's nostrils. Another method is to remove the skin of the dead foal and tie it over the orphan foal for 12 to 24 hours. The foster mother is then returned to the box and held firmly by the head. The orphan foal is introduced to her in such a way that she is prevented from kicking it. This may be done by holding the orphan foal, by having the mare's foreleg held up and by placing a twitch on the mare or giving her a tranquilliser. After allowing the mare to smell the foal, it is placed alongside her and allowed to suck. It is best to allow the mare to follow the foal round the box so that she may see it move. It is sometimes advisable to take the mare away from the foal for a short time. In this way the maternal instinct may be provoked. If the mare whinnies and shows distress at being taken away, it may be taken as a good sign that she will accept the orphan foal. Some mares, especially if they have stillborn foals and have not been suckled, have very little maternal instinct. After an hour or so it is usually fairly evident whether the mare is going to take the foal, although success may only be achieved after a much longer period. The two should not be left alone for several hours. The mare should be held in the box by someone, to make sure she will not attack or kick the foal.

There is no rule-of-thumb to tell whether a mare will make a good foster mother. Hot-tempered mares often have a strong maternal instinct and, once they accept the foal, become very good mothers. It is probably the sullen indifferent type which co-operate least and who are potentially the most dangerous so far as injury to the foal is concerned.

It may be that the mare has to be taken to the foal and, while this makes it more difficult, especially if the carcass of her own foal cannot also be taken with her, it is not impossible to achieve success. The application of an aromatic ointment to the mare's nostrils, such as one used for inhalation, overrides all other odours. Once the foster mother has accepted the foal, she will treat it as she would her own and there is no further cause for concern.

Why the foster mother accepts the orphan under any of these circumstances cannot be fully explained.

In practice, we do know that a proportion of mares will readily co-operate and that a proportion refuse, whatever is done.

If an orphan foal has not received the colostrum, or first milk, from its mother, it is important that it should receive some form of protection in another way. This can be done by giving a transfusion of blood plasma to the foal from a mare. The vet is able to transfer a number of antibodies which are contained in the circulating blood of all animals. It is also possible to give antibiotics for a number of days to reduce the risk of infection. Neither of these methods is as good as the natural protection afforded by colostrum.

23: The heat of the body

The animal kingdom can be divided, roughly speaking into two groups. The first comprises animals such as snakes, insects, lizards, tortoises, frogs, fishes, and so on, in which the body temperature varies with that of the surroundings. This group is usually referred to as 'cold-blooded'. The second group, known as 'warm-blooded', comprises all mammals, including, therefore, the horse.

Warm-blooded animals are so-called because they can maintain their body temperature whatever the outside conditions. Different species have differing normal temperatures (the elephant 96°F, humans 98°F, the horse 101°F and small birds 109°F). In each species, there may be variations of a degree or two above and below those figures but, however cold or hot the natural environment, the temperature of the body will be regulated so that it falls within narrow limits. The horse, as with other warm-blooded creatures, keeps its body temperature constant by a continual process in which the amount of heat produced within the body is balanced against the heat that is being lost to the outside. When the surroundings become very warm, heat loss is reduced. On the other hand, in the cold, heat loss is increased making the problem one of heat retention.

Heat is produced in the body when foodstuffs such as carbohydrates are burnt releasing energy in the form of heat. Heat is also produced when the muscles are used, adding to the heat which is continually being created from the normal chemical processes of life while the body is at rest. Heat loss is also a continual process, although the body incorporates mechanisms for regulating it, reducing loss in the cold and increasing it during periods of excess heat production, such as during exercise in warm weather.

Heat is lost in four different ways - by conduction, convection, evaporation or radiation. Conduction involves the transference of heat from one object to another by direct contact, as a hotplate transfers heat to a saucepan of milk. Thus, heat will pass by this means from a foal to the cold floor. Convection is the loss of heat by the movement of air around an object. In everyday language this process is usually called a draught although, if we blow hot air over an object which is at a lower temperature than that of the air, heat actually passes in the opposite direction, from the air to the body or object over which it is passing. Evaporation is a term used when heat is lost as a result of a liquid on the surface of a body turning from liquid to gas. This effect can easily be demonstrated by putting methylated spirit on the skin, the cooling effect due to evaporation being apparent. Radiation involves a transfer of heat from one body or object at a higher temperature to another at a lower temperature. In fact, all objects are continually exchanging heat by the process of radiating one to another, even across great distances or in a vacuum. The most obvious example of radiation is the warmth received from the sun, transferring energy in the form of heat (without which life as we know it could not exist). Radiation causes the heat of a foal in a loose box to be transferred to the colder objects of its surroundings, such as walls and windows.

Confining horses to boxes not only interferes with the natural process of heat production, but also exposes them to unnatural conditions in which heat loss may be greatly increased. It is one thing for a horse to be exposed to natural winds while in the paddock and free to move about, another to be exposed to the artificial winds of draughts within a box.

In hot weather, the animal may have difficulty in getting rid of its heat, especially when there is a lot of moisture in the atmosphere, lessening the effect of sweating, a potent method of heat loss as the fluid evaporates from the body surface. Under these adverse conditions the horse is able to reduce heat loss from the body surface in a most effective manner. The hair and fat beneath the surface of the skin forms a layer of insulation similar, in effect, to the artificial method used by humans in the form of clothing. In thin-skinned animals, such as those in training, when the amount of hair and natural dust within the coat are kept to a minimum by grooming and, in addition, the quantity of fat is reduced by exercise, clothes or rugs are placed on the horse's body to reduce heat loss. Besides using the insulation at the surface of its body, the horse can reduce the heat it loses by constricting the blood vessels beneath the surface of the skin so that less blood flows through them. After exercise or in warm weather, the vessels dilate and more blood passes through the surface layers, so that heat loss is increased. The adult horse, therefore, has little difficulty in adjusting the balance between heat production and heat loss so that the body temperature is kept within normal limits.

The position is very different in the young foal, especially in the first day of life. The foetus, as already noted, is kept in a private pool maintained at the body temperature of its mother until it arrives at birth in a cold and draughty box, soaked to the skin and having to regulate its body temperature for the first time, without any help from its mother. It is entirely dependent, in the first few hours of life, on the fuel reserves of food contained in the liver and other organs for the production of the heat necessary to offset the loss to its surroundings.

The foal loses heat by all four processes, but especially from the effects of evaporation of the amniotic fluid with which its coat is saturated and by radiation to the cold walls and windows of the box. It is, therefore, essential to make sure that the walls and ceilings of loose boxes are kept warm, which can only be done by good insulation, or by lining them with artificial means of supplying radiant heat. The effect of heat loss from the foal's body, popularly called chilling, can have serious consequences, making the animal more liable, among other illnesses, to diarrhoea and infections.

The part played by convection or draughts in disease of young stock is one which every owner should bear in mind when constructing new boxes or when improving those which are old. Boxes in which foals are born should be virtually draught-proof with an air temperature between 10-20ºC. This is below the temperature at which the foal expends least energy and it is important to ensure that the foal obtains sufficient colostrum and milk (energy). For a foal which is sick or small in size and which may therefore have inadequate energy reserves, it is necessary to maintain the air temperature at about 20°C. It is equally important for such foals to consume sufficient energy (for a normal foal weighing 50kg, this would be approximately 8-10l of milk per day) during the first week. Abrupt changes in air temperature should be avoided so, if the newborn foal is to go outside, the box should be cooled gradually and the foal only turned out if the weather is warm and/or sunny.

Under no circumstances, however, should the warmth of a foaling box be increased (for example, to about 30°C) so that the foal is unable to rid itself of the heat produced within its body. Very high air temperatures and moist, humid conditions may considerably distress the foal, just as it does the older animal, perhaps leading to respiratory infections and other disturbances in the body.

24: Meaning of inflammation

In the horse world there is a growing need, on the one hand, to explain scientific terminology and, on the other, to drop many older terms which have lost their usefulness. Otherwise, communication between vet and horse owner is likely to be difficult or confused.

The word 'inflammation' is a case in point. It describes a process which is present in most disease conditions, and is often used in day-to-day conversation whenever disease is being discussed. If a word ends in '-itis', it means 'inflammation of' that part of the body. Thus, 'tendonitis' means inflammation of the tendon, and 'conjunctivitis' inflammation of the conjunctiva. Since most parts of the body obtain their names from Latin or Greek, the seat of some conditions may be less obvious. Dermatitis is inflammation of the skin. Cystitis or otitis are probably best described as inflammation of the bladder and ear respectively. More common examples are peritonitis of the peritoneum and myocarditis of heart muscle.

Inflammation is a response of animal tissue to injury. Whatever the tissue (ie whether it is heart muscle, skin, tendon, and so on) and whatever the cause of the injury (eg by bacteria, viruses, burning, cutting, chemicals or parasites, and so on) the body responds in a characteristic way. The ancient Romans recognised the signs of inflammation which they described as redness, heat, swelling and pain.

Tissue injury, of course, means death of the cells and when the cells die they release the material which is normally contained within them. These substances, in turn, produce further effects on the undamaged cells surrounding the injury. The blood vessels in the area of the injury dilate, resulting in an increased quantity of blood to the affected part, and this accounts for the redness, swelling and heat. This increase in blood supply brings to the site of damage various white blood cells which are responsible for removing bacteria, debris and other matter which has been caused by the injury. In addition to the cells, fluid passes from the blood vessels and, in this way, an exudate is formed. The cells of the exudate have many functions. Some 'eat' the bacteria and digest them. Others produce enzymes which digest the dead tissue, while other types supply antibodies which kill the infective agents.

The purpose of the response of the body known as inflammation is thus the killing of any infective agents and the prevention of its spread into other parts of the body, the clearing up of dead cells, and, finally, the repair and restitution of the damaged area. Depending on the site of injury, the repair may be completed by regeneration of the neighbouring cells, such as happens in the skin, in the liver, and certain other organs. Some tissues, in particular nerve cells, cannot regenerate and scar tissue forms. Likewise when large areas of skin are affected.

Although the process of inflammation is basically the same in any part of the body, it varies to some extent with the nature or cause of the injury to the cells and also to the type of tissue that is affected. For instance, if the body receives a penetrating wound through the skin into the muscle beneath, it is easy to recognise the inflammatory response of increased blood supply to the area. If the wound becomes contaminated with bacteria, the process may continue with the formation of an abscess. The pus that forms in an abscess consists of the cells that are active during inflammation, together with the products of the dead cells which have been destroyed by the injury, and the bacteria.

When a tendon is sprained, the cause of inflammation is the tearing of tendon fibres and, as there is no open wound, contamination with bacteria does not take place. The inflammation of the tendon, however, takes the same general form as described and, although the blood supply to the tendon is much more limited than to skin and muscle, there is nevertheless an increased flow to the part, resulting in swelling, heat and pain.

When the structures associated with joints are sprained or knocked, an identical sequence of events is seen and felt. If the inflammation affects the internal lining of the joint, it is often referred to as arthritis. An arthritis may be categorised as infective, rheumatic or traumatic, depending on the cause.

As noted, bacteria, viruses and other infective agents may cause inflammation in the internal organs of the body and, although it is not so easily recognised, it is nevertheless the same process. The abscesses which are formed in the kidney of a newborn foal after infection with BVE (*Bacteria viscosum equi*) and pneumonia, often termed 'inflammation of the lung', are examples.

Finally, an explanation of the terms peritonitis and adhesions.

In the abdominal cavity, the gut coils upon itself many times and the coils lie side by side. The outside of the wall of the tube is covered by a thin, shiny membrane, called the peritoneum. This membrane also lines the inside of the walls of the abdominal cavity formed by the muscles of the abdomen, flank and back. Inflammation of this membrane may result from a blood clot cutting off the blood supply to a small portion of bowel wall, resulting in cell death. The same inflammatory response is then seen as in other parts of the body. This is known as peritonitis and, in repair, the scar tissue formed may attach itself to neighbouring parts of the peritoneum and in this way adhesions are formed between two loops of bowel or between the bowel and the abdominal wall. Peritonitis and adhesions are also seen after surgical operations and sometimes from infection.

Treatment is virtually always directed at the cause and effects of inflammation. The cause is attacked by using antibiotics if it is an infective condition and the process of inflammation speeded up by applying heat, bringing more blood to the area. As this may cause congestion, alternate hot and cold applications may be used. The latter, by reducing blood flow, also helps reduce pain and swelling. There are also many drugs available today which specifically combat the degree of inflammation and limit the effect of injury.

25: The breathing apparatus

Every trainer fears the sight of a trickle of blood issuing from the nostrils of one of his horses after it has done a gallop. He knows this may be the forerunner of a full scale nosebleed. Blood may then pour (in a deluge) down both nostrils, spattering the rider if the horse happens to be galloping. If a horse suffers from this type of haemorrhage, it can usually be expected to recur. The racing careers of many well-known horses have thus been abruptly terminated. Such a horse is often referred to as a 'bleeder', while the technical name given to nosebleed is 'epistaxis'.

What causes a horse to have nosebleed? The blood that issues from the nostrils, whether it is a trickle or a stream, must come from a leakage from the walls of a blood vessel at some part of the air passages, which extend from the nostrils to the lungs. The air passages consist of two nasal passages in the head extending from the nostrils to the pharynx, then forming a single tube (the windpipe), the upper part of which forms the larynx (Fig 25.1). The windpipe divides at its lower end in the chest supplying a branch to each lung. These branches in turn divide into many smaller tubes which eventually connect with the air sacs or alveoli. If the haemorrhage comes from one of the two nasal passages in the head, the blood will most probably discharge from one nostril only. But if, as is more often the case, its origin is between the throat and lungs, the blood will then be seen at both nostrils.

There is considerable variation in the quantity of blood lost, depending on the size of the vessel from which the bleeding occurs and the degree of damage to its wall. In some individuals there is only a trickle, while at the other extreme, the haemorrhage will be so profuse that it causes the death of the animal. In most cases, the reason why a blood vessel 'breaks' is unknown, although exercise may play some part. This is known as exercise-induced pulmonary haemorrhage (EIPH). This is not surprising since blood pressure rises during exertion and more blood is therefore passing through the vessels of the lungs and those in the lining of the air passages.

Some evidence is available from post-mortem examinations of horses that drop dead from haemorrhage or of bleeders which are put down for one reason or another. The rupture of a blood vessel is sometimes found to be associated with a patch of inflammation or pneumonia in the lungs. It would be interesting to know if there are more bleeders following widespread coughing epidemics.

Another known cause of haemorrhage is when an ulcer forms in the linings of the air passages and erodes one of the blood vessels which lie either within the lining or even at some distance underneath. These ulcers may occur at any point along the air passages, but there is one position in which they have frequently been found, that is in one of the two guttural pouches (see Fig 25.1 for explanation of this term) in horses affected with profuse nosebleeds. These usually occur spontaneously and not following exercise. They may therefore be differentiated from exercise-induced pulmonary haemorrhage. A large tributary of the carotid artery runs through the roof of the pouch and it is therefore unsurprising to find that the ulcer has 'eaten' into the wall of the artery, causing profuse and sometimes fatal haemorrhage.

When bleeding occurs, the blood escapes into the pouch and from there passes into the pharynx and down one, or both, of the nostrils. The pouch itself may become filled with blood and a swelling will then appear behind the angle of the jaw on the side on which the bleeding is occurring. Unlike the bleeder in which haemorrhage occurs only at exercise, the bleeding from the pouch more often starts when the horse is at rest. In some cases there may be an association between ulceration and symptoms such as difficulty in swallowing, or paralysis of the soft palate and vocal chords. The reason is that the nerves supplying the muscles which control those parts are close to the roof of the pouch and may become damaged by the inflammation associated with the ulcer in its active stage or by the scar tissue which is left behind when it heals. Many different treatments have been tried in attempts to cure horses which suffer from nosebleeds. While optimistic claims have been made for many such treatments, most vets would agree that, apart from the obvious necessity to rest a horse if the bleeding is associated with galloping, no one treatment ever achieves consistent results.

Before deciding on what treatment should be applied to any particular individual, it is first necessary to try to find out which is the point of origin of the bleeding. Also, if there is any indication as to cause. Employing an instrument known as an endoscope it is possible to take a look at the lining of the upper part of the air passages, as far as the lungs. An endoscope consists of a flexible tube in which a system of fibres conveys light and images back to the viewer. In this way, can be seen the guttural pouches and the airways to the position where they become too small as they break up into fine tubes in the lung itself.

The history of the case must also be taken into consideration. Does the bleeding occur after exercise or only at rest? Are there any symptoms of swelling or pain or pressure at any place along the air passages and especially in the region of the guttural pouches? Symptoms of infection, such as a discharge of mucus or pus from the nose, or an increase in the number of white cells circulating in the blood, must

The breathing apparatus   *101*

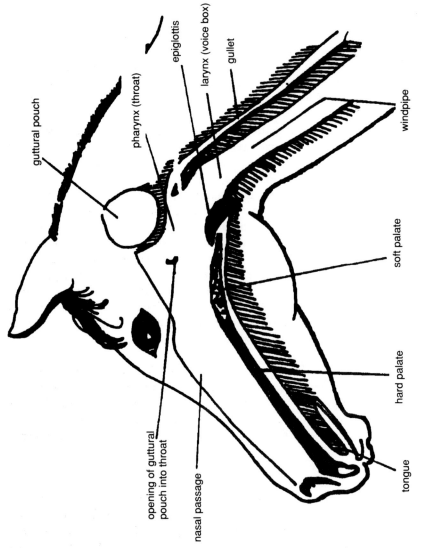

guttural pouch

pharynx (throat)

epiglottis

larynx (voice box)

gullet

windpipe

soft palate

hard palate

tongue

opening of guttural pouch into throat

nasal passage

Fig 25.1: Air passages

102

The breathing apparatus

also be taken into account.

Of the drugs that have been used over the years in treatment, the most popular have been Vitamins C and K, together with drugs which, in theory at least, are said to increase the tendency of the blood to coagulate. Lasix, a diuretic, has become popular as a treatment of bleeders in the USA. There is no direct evidence that these diuretics reduce bleeding episodes although their continued use suggests that practitioners and trainers have some faith in them. In the UK, it is not permitted to use such drugs before a race and diuretics have not, therefore, been tested in practice in this country. Anti-inflammatory drugs and antibiotics have also been used in cases where infection has been suspected of being the original cause of the weakness of the blood vessel.

If an ulcer can be seen, such as the one described in the guttural pouch, it is possible to treat this by direct application of various antibiotic and healing drugs. A recent procedure has been to tie the branch of the carotid artery under general anaesthetic and a surgical operation.

Apart from those cases where infection is clearly indicated (*eg* influenza virus), the exact cause of the bleeding is never easy to diagnose. A local infection of the lining of the air passages, damage arising from the head being knocked, the inhalation of foreign bodies setting up an inflammatory reaction, are all possibilities which have been suggested at one time or another. The question is also asked whether bleeders have inherited their condition. However, without support from statistical evidence, it is better that suggestions, such as these should be assumed to be untrue until proved otherwise. If inheritance does play a part in bleeding, it could only be in a very small percentage of individuals. We should not, therefore, condemn a stallion because he himself has been a confirmed bleeder while in training.

What of the future? Is improvement likely in the results that can be obtained from the treatment of bleeders? It is unlikely that there will be any spectacular progress because the bleeding is merely a symptom of what is probably a number of different conditions. However, improvements in the treatment of certain types of these conditions, as our knowledge of their actual cause becomes established, can be expected.

Gone in the wind

The term 'wind' is often applied to the whole process of breathing, which involves the movement of air in and out of the air passages and lungs. When people speak of a horse having 'gone in its wind' they may be referring to broken wind, but the term is more commonly used when there is an obstruction to the air flow at some point in the air passages. Depending on the nature of such obstruction, and the abnormal sounds that occur during breathing as a direct result, the horse may be said to 'whistle', 'roar', 'grunt' or 'gurgle'.

When the chest wall expands, air is drawn into the lungs just as it is into a pair of bellows. This process of inspiration alternates with a contraction of the chest which expels the air from the lungs (expiration). In a horse, the distance from the start of the passages, at the nose, to the lung is relatively great when compared with the human, due to the elongated head and neck. The exchange of the gas oxygen from air (which contains about 20 per cent) to bloodstream takes place in the air sacs of the lungs. During the two phases of breathing, ie inspiration and expiration, by no means is all the air expelled from the lungs. It is as if a column of air is being continually pushed up and pulled down the air passages, allowing for the mixing of the oxygen-rich air with the gas in the air sacs. These start at the nostrils and continue as the nasal passages through the head to the throat. Here the air has to cross the food passage into the larynx, which is a box-like structure at the top of the windpipe (trachea). The windpipe continues down the neck into the chest where it divides into two, one branch supplying each of the two lungs.

The comparatively great length of the horse's air passages has already been noted. There is an enormous increase in air flow down these passages with greater exertion. The size of the air passages is normally quite adequate to meet the requirements of the horse when it is galloping at full stretch, but there are certain portions which have to be dilated when the air flow is increased. This is achieved by the action of certain muscles which increase the diameter during the time that air is being breathed in.

To appreciate fully this point, the reader need only watch a horse's nostrils at the end of a gallop. At this time they will be seen to be widely dilating as the horse breathes in.

The other part of the air passages which dilates in a rather similar fashion during exercise, and to a much lesser extent at rest, are certain structures in the larynx. The latter comprises the entrance to the windpipe and also forms the floor of the throat, over which food passes into the gullet at the time of swallowing. One of the functions of the larynx, therefore, is to prevent food from passing the wrong way. Besides this action during swallowing, it also has a part to play when particles of dust are breathed in through the nose. The opening into the larynx can be enlarged or reduced by the movement of the vocal cords (Fig 25.2). These structures lie across the path of the air and unless they are pulled aside during inspiration they will cause a partial obstruction. The muscles which pull them to one side when the horse breathes in are under nervous control which synchronises their movement with inspiration. The fact that they return towards the midline when the horse breathes out does not impede the outflow of air as, by their shape, they act as a kind of valve, restricting inflow but allowing outflow.

When the muscle supplying the vocal cords becomes paralysed and they are not pulled back in the normal manner, the entry of air into the windpipe will be impeded. The greater the airflow, as in exercise, the more pronounced the effect. The rush of air past this obstruction sets up a noise which can be heard with varying clarity, depending on the degree of obstruction and the volume of air which is

The breathing apparatus

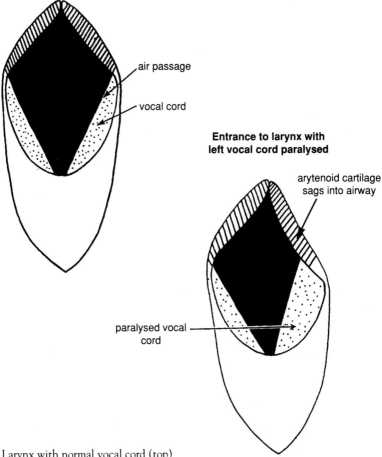

Entrance to normal larynx viewed from throat

air passage

vocal cord

Entrance to larynx with left vocal cord paralysed

arytenoid cartilage sags into airway

paralysed vocal cord

Fig 25.2: Larynx with normal vocal cord (top) and larynx with paralysed vocal cord (bottom)

passing. The noise usually becomes loudest at exercise. It is for this reason that in examinations for soundness a horse is always galloped in order to diagnose this particular ailment. On these occasions, the noise that is heard occurs only during inspiration because, as noted, the valve-like nature of the cords allows for the free exit, but not entry, of air.

The noise varies in its quality, but is usually harsh and high-pitched (hence the term 'whistling'). It may be very faint or heard at a distance of many yards when the horse is galloping. Using an endoscope, it is possible in the stable to see the vocal

The breathing apparatus

cords being pulled apart, helping to confirm diagnosis. Endoscopes can be used after a horse has pulled up from the gallop and this provides the opportunity of viewing the vocal cords when they are in their most active state. Defects can then be seen more clearly than when the horse is examined at rest. It is nearly always the left cord that is affected, for reasons which are not fully understood. It may be due to the rather longer route which the nerve to the left follows compared with the nerve supply to the right.

How does this partial obstruction in the larynx of the horse affect the horse's performance? There are many variable factors involved. In many individuals that suffer from this disease, the amount of air that can enter the windpipe even at a time of full exertion is adequate for the needs of the animal. On the other hand, if a critical point is reached and there is insufficient supply, the animal will not be able to give its best performance. Furthermore, if this continues, it may well mean that the heart will be affected and serious consequences of a permanent nature may well ensue.

An operation to remove the vocal cords will in most cases remove the obstruction and, if the performance of the horse has been limited because of the paralysis, the subsequent improvement may be spectacular. The operation is generally known after one of the early pioneers of its use, Professor Hobday. It consists of opening the larynx from the outside of the throat and removing part of the cords, so that after healing they are virtually obliterated. They cannot then cause an obstruction even though their muscle is paralysed. A more recent variation of the Hobday operation is to employ a 'tieback'. This consists of inserting an elastic band into the cartilage which support the vocal cords and thereby anchoring the whole cartilage to one side.

The symptom of an unusual noise during the breathing of a horse does not necessarily mean that the sound or noise is from a paralysed vocal cord. Air flowing past any obstruction in the air passages is liable to result in an unusual sound, so that tumours, abscesses and inflamed areas at any point in the air passages may also be responsible. Paralysis of the soft palate may cause the gurgling sound which is often thought to be associated with swallowing the tongue. The soft palate forms a part of the throat and is therefore a structure closely associated with the swallowing mechanism, being partly responsible for the division of the air passages from those containing food. When swallowing occurs, breathing automatically stops, and vice versa.

Many suggestions have been put forward over the years as to the cause of vocal cord paralysis and, more recently, of soft palate paralysis in the horse. The most commonly supported views are those that favour inheritance and the action of toxins following infection, such as strangles. There can be no doubt that inheritance plays a part in some cases and it is well known that certain breeding lines are susceptible to this type of wind infirmity.

For this reason, in many breeds soundness of wind is required before a stallion is

The breathing apparatus

granted a licence to stand at stud. This does not apply to thoroughbreds kept for stud purposes in the racing industry.

26: The eye of the horse

Most people would probably agree that sight is the most precious of all the senses. The horse, however, relies more on hearing and smell for its appreciation of what is going on around it.

The eyes function on much the same principle as a camera. Light enters through a lens which focuses an image on the film at the back of the camera, thereby causing certain chemical changes to take place within the film. The eye has a lens which, by changing its shape, focuses an image on the retina at the back of the eye (Fig 26.1). The retina is a sensitive membrane which transmits this image in the form of nerve impulses through the optic nerve to the brain. The brain interprets the impulses in a form we call 'sight'. The amount of light passing through the lens is regulated by the pupil, which alters its diameter according to whether it is receiving dull or bright light, in a manner similar to the way the shutter of a camera is manipulated. Muscles are attached to the outer surface of the eyeballs so that they can move in various directions, thus increasing the field of vision. The movements of the eyes are co-ordinated to focus on the same point at any one time.

The reader can refer to Figure 26.1 for a general idea of how the different parts of the eyeball are arranged. The eyeball is set in a bony cavity of the skull known as the orbit, protected in front by the eyelids and their lining, the conjunctiva. At the back it is covered by layers of fibre and fat, amongst which can be found the small muscles which are responsible for movement. The eyeball is not a true sphere, but flattened in front. It is prevented from collapsing by the fluid which is contained inside the tough outer shell consisting of the sclera (white of the eye) and the cornea. The lens divides the interior of the eyeball into the front and back chambers.

The horse possesses a fold of the conjunctiva at an inner angle of the eye which is known as the third eyelid. When a horse has tetanus or lockjaw, the third eyelid flickers across the eyeball, especially when the face is tapped lightly. Underneath the lids are lachrymal glands which continually supply fluid to lubricate and wash the front of the eyeball. This fluid drains away through a duct running beneath the skin between the eye and the nostrils. If the glands produce an excess of fluid as may happen when the eyeball is irritated by injury or if the draining duct becomes blocked, the fluid overflows and tears run down the face.

The various parts of the eye and its associated structures (the eyelids, conjunctivae, and so on) may become diseased and these conditions or diseases are often referred to by the Latin name derived from the part that is affected (conjunctivitis, scleritis, and so forth). The eyelids of the horse may be torn by nails, hooks, barbed wire or other hazards or as the result of a kick from another animal. The result of such injuries is much the same as in other parts of the body, swelling and inflammation - a horse's black eye! Just as with other cuts, it may be necessary to suture the edges of these lacerations so that healing takes place more easily.

In foals, the lower eyelid may become turned inwards, causing the outer surface or skin to rub directly on to the eyeball, so that its surface becomes injured. This condition, known as entropion, may follow from rubbing on the straw bedding during bouts of pain, as in meconium stoppages. In some cases, the animal may be born with the eyelids turned in and, in any condition where there is a loss of body fluid (such as diarrhoea), the fat behind the eyeball may shrink, so that the whole eyeball sinks further into the orbit and the lower eyelids therefore turn inwards. For treatment, turning out the eyelids from time to time may be resorted to until the underlying cause is successfully treated. At times it is necessary to put temporary sutures in the skin to pull the eyelid outwards for several days.

The lining of the eyelids may become inflamed (conjunctivitis) as a result of infection with bacteria or viruses, by foreign bodies such as grit or mud landing on the surface, or from certain types of allergy. A malignant tumour may grow from the third eyelid, and many of these have been successfully treated by surgery and the application of radioactive substances.

Many of the conditions that affect the eyelids also damage the surface of the eyeball, that is the sclera and cornea. Injury to these surfaces results in the formation of ulcers and eventually, as healing takes place, scars will appear. If an ulcer or injury penetrates through all the layers of the outer capsule of the eyeball, the fluid inside may escape, and the eyeball will then collapse.

The internal structures of the eyeball may also become diseased or injured and one of the best known is periodic ophthalmia, or 'moon blindness'. The cause of the condition is not known for certain, although many theories have been put forward over the years. Infection with bacteria, virus or certain worms have been held responsible, while another suggestion claims the condition is the result of an allergy. A horse suffering from moon blindness shows signs of a catarrhal inflammation of the conjunctivae, and a marked dislike of light in the affected eye. The eyelids are half-closed, especially when a bright light is shone into the eye, the pupil contracting in an attempt to shut out as much light as possible, while the pupil in the unaffected eye remains widely open. There may be a slight rise in temperature, but the animal does not usually show any general illness. Very often, the condition appears to respond to treatment or clears up spontaneously, and the owner believes that the horse has been hit in the eye or that there is some other simple explanation for the inflammation. However, at varying intervals, the condition recurs, perhaps with more severity each time, until eventually permanent changes occur within the eyeball and the animal becomes blind. These changes include the formation of adhesions between the iris or pupil and the lens, the appearance of cataracts in the lens, and the loss of fluid in the eyeball, causing it to

The eye of the horse

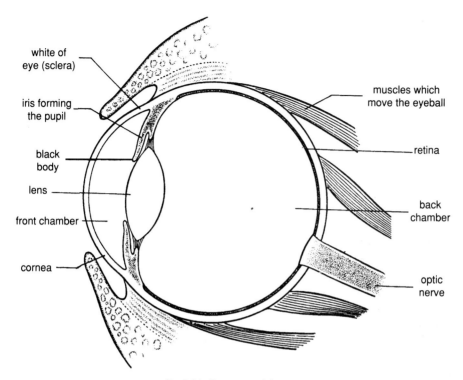

white of eye (sclera)

iris forming the pupil

black body

lens

front chamber

cornea

muscles which move the eyeball

retina

back chamber

optic nerve

Fig 26.1: Structure of the eye

collapse partially. One or sometimes both eyes may suffer the same fate. Many treatments have been tried, including antibiotics and corticosteroids, but there is no form of therapy which will definitely prevent or cure the condition.

A scar or cataract formed in any of the ways mentioned above may interfere with the passage of light through the eyeball to the retina. The effect that it has depends on size and position.

When a horse or a foal suffers from a debilitating disease such as strangles, pus cells may collect in the front chamber of the eye, causing the lower part to cloud. Such clouding may appear and disappear quite suddenly as the general condition of the animal improves.

Every year a small number of foals are born with one or both eyes missing. It is not known whether such cases are the result of a viral infection of the mother during the early stages of pregnancy, the administration of drugs during this period or from inheritance.

Much more could be written about the eye. However, the above outline should give the horse owner a basic understanding of how the eye functions and in what ways it is likely to be damaged or diseased. Many modern drugs are available for the

The eye of the horse

treatment of such conditions and owners are well-advised to call in their veterinary surgeons at an early stage to avoid unfortunate consequences.

27: How the kidneys work

The bloodstream acts as a transport system, taking digested foodstuffs to all the cells of the body. At the same time waste material is carried away in the blood to be excreted. This elimination, or excretion, of unwanted material is the responsibility of several organs. For instance, the lungs remove excess gas, the gut a proportion of solid substances, and the kidneys various salts dissolved in water, the solution known as urine.

The amount of urine passed by a horse during 24 hours varies considerably under differing conditions of management and feeding. As a rough guide, ten pints might be an average. Urine plays an important part in veterinary medicine because of the relatively large quantities in which it is excreted from the body and the fact that it can be collected and analysed in laboratories. Urine analysis in clinical medicine has long been an aid in the diagnosis of many diseases. Its use for the diagnosis of pregnancy from about 130 days of gestation onwards is also well-known. A more recent innovation is the testing of urine and saliva for the presence of drugs.

To make full use of urine analysis in the diagnosis of disease, it is necessary not only to recognise what are normal or abnormal contents, but also understand the purpose and method of its formation within the body. The urinary organs consist of those which actually produce the urine, namely the two kidneys, and those responsible for conveying the fluid to the exterior so that it may be expelled from the body (Figs 27.1, and 27.2). The two kidneys in the horse lie on either side of the body, approximately midway between the withers and the croup. They are to be found deep to the spine or vertebral column and the great muscle mass of the back.

In this position they are well protected from external injury and it is therefore most uncommon for them to become bruised. Their shape is not identical, one being roughly in the form of a bean and the other similar in shape to the heart of a playing card. In the adult, each weighs 20-25oz and measures about 6-7in in length.

Once the urine has been formed in the kidney, it passes down a tube or duct known as the ureter. These two tubes take the fluid into the bladder where it collects until the time when it is expelled to the outside, often known in the horse as 'staling'. The bladder is a hollow organ with muscular walls, capable of great distension so that it may contain as much as a gallon of urine. A single channel of exit known as a urethra connects the bladder with the external urinary orifice.

One function of the kidneys is to clear the bloodstream of certain salts and waste material in the manner of a filter. At the same time while keeping the bloodstream 'clean', it must not allow protein, blood cells, sugar and other vital substances of the bloodstream to pass out in the urine with the unwanted material. A further

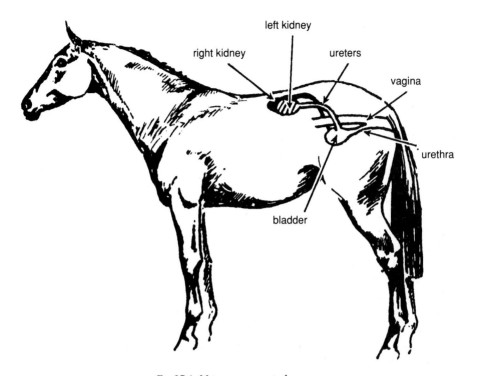

Fig 27.1: Urinary organs in horse

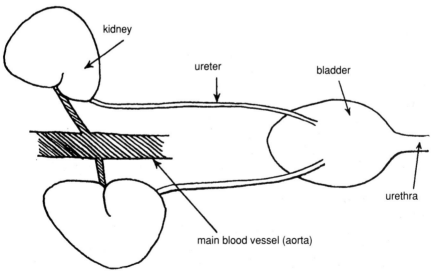

Fig 27.2: Close-up of main organs

How the kidneys work

function is the elimination or conservation of water within the body according to present needs. For example, if there is excess water in the tissues the kidneys will pass more urine. Conversely, the volume can be drastically reduced if insufficient fluid is available and the body is dehydrated. Various substances which enter the body in diet or, exceptionally, by injection may also be eliminated from the bloodstream through the kidneys. The chemist makes use of this knowledge when analysing urine for the presence of 'dope'.

The kidneys enable the body to dispose of certain natural substances which, were they allowed to accumulate in abnormally high concentrations, would act as a poison to the organism as a whole. The kidneys are composed of a million or so small individual units called nephrons, each acting as a filter. Each nephron consists of a capillary blood vessel closely associated with a urinary duct or two. The latter have blind ends and, after making a U-turn, drain into a common channel with their fellows. In this way, the urine which forms within the tube is eventually expelled from the kidney into the ureter. The arrangement between the blood vessel and the urinary duct is so intimate that substances can pass easily from the blood into the tubes. The cells lining the tubes are capable of a high degree of selection, so that they dictate which substances should pass and which should not. In this way the composition of the urine can be controlled in a manner which ensures that vital substances, such as blood cells are not lost in the urine while, at the same time, the necessary elimination of waste products can be achieved. The quantity of urine which is formed and which therefore passes to the exterior is also

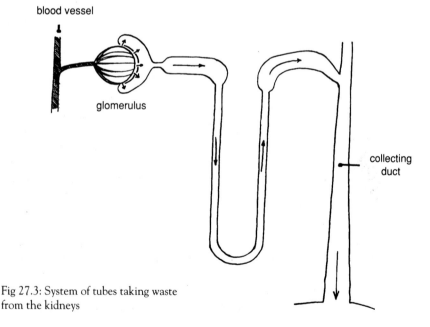

blood vessel

glomerulus

collecting duct

Fig 27.3: System of tubes taking waste from the kidneys

How the kidneys work

controlled by the tubes of the nephrons.

To illustrate this process, imagine a glass funnel over which a handkerchief has been spread. If water containing some beads were poured into the top of the funnel, the water would pass through the handkerchief and down the stem of the funnel, leaving the beads behind. The beads can be likened to material which is retained in the blood, while the water represents the fluid and dissolved substances which pass out through the filter in the kidney as urine. The stem of the funnel is the tube of the kidney nephron which leads to the ureter and so, through the bladder, to the exterior.

Of course, the process is much more complicated in reality than in the analogy. The living cells which line the blood vessels and the tubes of the kidney itself select, not only which substances should pass out from the bloodstream, but also the quantities of each. The amount and composition of urine is controlled by many complex influences, including the concentration of the various salts, electrolytes, and other material within the bloodstream. In addition, certain hormones from the pituitary and the adrenal glands play a part in the regulation of the composition and amount of urine voided at any time. Various drugs, called diuretics, act on the kidneys increasing the quantity of fluid passed. Such drugs can therefore be used in the treatment of those conditions where artificial withdrawal of water from the body is called for.

Diseases of the urinary system fall broadly into three categories. Thus, the main source of trouble may be in the bloodstream, while the kidneys and the ducts that take the urine from the body may be quite normal. Secondly, the kidney itself may be diseased. Thirdly, the bloodstream and the kidneys may be quite normal, but the excretory ducts - the ureter, bladder and urethra - diseased.

Red-coloured urine

In haemolytic jaundice of the newborn there is a massive destruction of red cells in the foal's bloodstream during the first 72 hours of life. The red pigment, known as haemoglobin, which is contained in the cells, is liberated in large quantities. It passes through the kidneys into the urine, causing the latter to turn a dark red colour.

Reddish-coloured urine may also be passed by animals suffering from 'set fast' or 'tying up'. In this condition, sometimes referred to as azoturia, the muscles of the back quarters become hard and painful. In extreme cases, a red pigment known as myoglobulin enters the bloodstream from the muscles and so, through the kidneys, into the urine.

Red urine is also seen after the common worm remedy of phenothiazine has been given to an animal. The drug is altered in its passage through the body and is eventually excreted from the kidney as a red dye. It is quite normal, therefore, for the urine to turn red some hours after an animal has received a dose. This may stain the buttocks red, especially in grey animals, and is sometimes taken to be blood.

Another example of abnormal substances appearing in the urine, not as a result of kidney disease but because of an alteration in the composition of the bloodstream, is diabetes. This disease does not usually affect the horse but is, of course, well known in humans. It is mentioned here because it illustrates how a disease in any part of the body may indirectly affect the kidneys and, so, the urine. In diabetes, the gland of the pancreas is diseased and insufficient insulin is produced in the body. In the absence of insulin there is an enormous increase in the sugar content. The cells which line the tubes of the kidney can select the substances which are to be retained in the blood and those which are to be passed to the outside in the urine. Sugar is one of those substances which is retained under normal circumstances, but in diabetes the concentration in the bloodstream becomes so high that large amounts are allowed through the kidneys and are therefore lost in the urine, which normally contains none.

Inflammation of the ducts taking urine from the kidneys

When there is infection or inflammation in the bladder or urethra the terms 'cystitis' and 'urethritis' are sometimes used. In these cases, abnormal substances such as pus cells and protein may be added to the urine as it passes on its way. Infection in the bladder and urethra are not frequently found in the horse. They are probably more common in the stallion than in the mare and the part played by infection in the urethra of the stallion, causing low fertility, is one which merits further investigation.

Stones or calculi may form in the bladder as a result of the accumulation of salts. These stones, once they start to form, often snowball to a relatively large size. Apart from irritating the lining of the bladder they may cause obstruction in the urethra. In all these conditions where there is an inflammation of the urinary canal there will be a painful sensation and a desire to urinate. Urination will therefore occur and will frequently be accompanied by pain, which the horse will show by grunting, uneasiness, swishing the tail and perhaps kicking at its belly. Diagnosis depends on the symptoms and examination of the urine, together with rectal palpation to detect the presence of stones.

It is important to distinguish between the different conditions which affect the urinary system. The presence of blood, pus cells and other substances not normally present in the urine, gives some indication that all is not well. Examination of the blood for the presence, in abnormally high concentrations, of substances usually eliminated by the kidney is also helpful. One such substance is urea which, if it accumulates in the bloodstream in exceptional quantities, causes a condition known as uraemia.

When a horse repeatedly adopts the position of urine passing, as is frequently seen in cases of colic, kidney disease is often mistakenly suspected. It is true that pain and frequent attempts at urination are seen when the bladder and urethra are inflamed, but these conditions are relatively rare, and the colic is nearly always the result of some intestinal upset.

Kidney diseases

There are certain tests which can be carried out to assess whether the kidney is functioning properly. These tests are performed on the blood and the urine, providing some indication of failure in kidney function. X-ray examination of the kidney is difficult in the horse but the use of ultrasound has enormously enlarged veterinary capabilities for diagnosing kidney disease, especially when stones, cysts or tumours are present. In addition, it is possible to feel the kidneys by rectal palpation and so gain an idea of whether or not they are of normal size.

In the horse, disease of the kidney itself is not as common as in other species such as ourselves or the dog. It may, however, be more common than we suspect, its comparative rareness being attributable rather to a failure to diagnose any such condition during life.

When the kidney fails to function properly, the results to the body may be serious. Salts, acids, and other substances which are normally taken from the blood may accumulate in high concentrations, so acting as a poison to the central nervous system and other parts of the body. Further, damage to the kidney may result in protein and similar vital substances passing through the filter of the kidney and being lost to the body in the urine. Such accumulations and losses to the bloodstream through the kidney may result from kidney damage caused by many different types of bacteria, parasites and poisons.

Abscesses may also form in the kidneys of foals suffering from 'sleepy foal disease' in the first few days of life or in older animals suffering from strangles infection. Damage may be caused by toxins which come to the kidney as a result of bacteria breeding in other parts of the body. Many of these cause inflammation of the blood vessels and tubes of the kidney.

Arsenic and other metals, together with overdoses of certain drugs, such as sulphonamides, may also cause damage.

The migrating larvae of the redworm, *strongylus vulgaris*, have been known to damage the blood vessels of the kidney. For this and other reasons, blood clots may form in some of the small arteries, so cutting off the blood supply to a portion of the kidney. The area of dead tissue thus caused is known to the pathologist as an infarct and may seriously reduce the ability of the kidney to function properly.

One condition which is well known to horsemen is that of 'box flooding' or polyuria. One or many individuals in a stable may suddenly start passing very large quantities of dilute urine. The affected animals all develop a great thirst and instead of drinking one bucket of water, two, three or perhaps more will be consumed in 24 hours. The condition lasts a few days or weeks and is generally associated with loss of form and bodily condition. In some cases, the animal may go off its feed for a short period and there may also be a small rise in temperature. The urine is very dilute - the amount of solid material is greatly reduced relative to water content - but it does not normally contain any abnormal substances. There are a number of theories concerning the cause of this condition. The feeding of certain types of oats or those of bad quality is blamed from time to time. Another theory is that a virus is responsible. It may well be that not all outbreaks have the same cause and that both theories are in some measure correct.

Further investigation into this condition is needed, so that it can be properly diagnosed, cured and its occurrence eventually prevented.

28: Problems of equine nutrition

Until recently, so little was known about the nutritional requirements of a horse that almost anyone who wished to do so could consider himself an expert.

The reason for this lack of knowledge was that there was little interest in the species compared with cattle and sheep, a more profitable area for farm feedstock suppliers. This meant that comparatively little research was carried out on horses. Further, nutritional research on horses is particularly expensive to carry out. However, during the last decade, there has been an increasing amount of information gathered about horses and their nutritional requirements, the study of which has been placed on a rather more scientific basis than previously.

Napoleon supposedly once said that 'an army marches on its stomach'. Similarly, a horse must surely gallop on its caecum and colon, its most important digestive organs. A young horse cannot be expected to develop into a fine adult specimen if it does not receive the correct nourishment during the time that it is growing or while it is being carried in its mother. Nor can we expect top performances from racehorses, show jumpers, hunters or ponies, if the diet they are fed does not contain the necessary ingredients to sustain them in their work.

The following explanation of the general principles involved in horse nutrition are intended as a general introduction to a complex subject. In particular, it should bring greater understanding to the purchase of fodder and the various proprietary mixes of vitamins, minerals and so on.

There are three basic considerations to take into account: the digestive processes of the horse, the components which make up what we loosely describe as food, and the particular requirements of the horse for these under varying conditions of its life.

First, a cautionary word, relevant to the first and last of these categories. Present day methods of feeding and the composition of rations fed to horses are based largely on traditional lines or on knowledge acquired from other species, such as cattle, sheep, and even ourselves. It is often misleading, even dangerous, to assume that we can use the information acquired from the study of another species without first having carried out the basic research necessary to discover if the horse is exceptional in any particular respect. For example, to say that a horse requires any particular vitamin because the human suffers if it is not included in diet, may or may not be true.

What is digestion? The term refers to the various processes to which food is subjected as it passes along the gut of the horse. Such processes must take place before the different nutritional substances can be converted into a suitable form for absorption through the wall of the gut into the bloodstream, so that the body can make use of them.

For the purpose of digestion, the horse, as other animals, is provided with a digestive system which is referred to as the alimentary canal, or more often as the guts or intestines. This canal consists of a very long tube beginning at the mouth and ending at the anus, enlarging at various portions to form the organs called the stomach, caecum and so on. The gullet or oesophagus passes the food from the mouth to the stomach, and from there it travels to the small and large intestines which extract the nutritional parts of the food while the undigested residue is passed out of the anus as dung.

The nutritive portion of foodstuffs consists of protein, fat and carbohydrates (to be explained later). These are made available to the animal in a number of ways. In the first place, food is ground by the chewing action of the teeth and, mixed with saliva, it is swallowed into the stomach. From there, as it passes along the tube, it is mixed with the digestive juices secreted by the lining of the gut or by various glands, such as the liver and the pancreas. In addition, in the horse, bacteria play a major role in breaking down foodstuffs.

The movements (peristalsis) of the gut wall propels the food from one end of the gut to the other and also ensures a thorough mixing of the contents. The horse has a relatively small stomach (its capacity is about the same as that of the sheep) and a voluminous large intestine, divided into three distinct portions called the caecum, the colon, and the rectum. The caecum resembles a balloon in the shape of a comma, with an inlet from the small intestine and an outlet to the colon placed close together, near to one end. The colon is about ten inches wide, but narrows to a U-shape, in its middle part about four inches, and it is here that stoppages occur in some cases of colic.

A close relationship can be seen in every animal between the structure of its teeth, the digestive tract, and the type of food that it eats. The horse, with its comparatively small stomach, is accustomed to eating a small amount of food at frequent intervals, and the teeth are shaped to chew fibrous matter, such as hay, or to crush grain. This is in contrast to the dog, say, whose teeth are adapted in shape for tearing flesh. The development of the caecum and colon to an enormous capacity of 30 gallons (compared with 4 gallons for the stomach) allows for the bacterial fermentation as necessary for the digestion of cellulose and fibre.

From the process of digestion, the horse obtains protein, carbohydrate, sugar, vitamins, and minerals.

Proteins are complex molecules formed by living cells from simpler molecules known as amino acids. They are found in every living cell so that, if the water is removed from the soft tissues of the body (muscle, skin, etc) the dry matter remaining would consist of 80 per cent or so of various proteins. There is only a small number (about 20) of different amino acids from which proteins are composed, although there are very many different proteins. Amino acids are arranged in the protein molecule in long chains, often 100 or more, much as beads are arranged on a string. Since the sequence in which the amino acids are joined and the manner in which they fold are responsible for the character of the protein, the number of possible variations of form and function are practically unlimited. Both plants and animals can build amino acids into protein for their own tissues, but only plants are able to form the necessary amino acids from simpler substances. For this reason, so-called 'essential' amino acids must be obtained either by eating plants, which have originally made them, or the flesh of an animal which has previously eaten those plants. The horse, feeding as it does entirely on plants, obtains its essential amino acids by the first method.

Carbohydrates are another of the major groups of substances of which living matter is composed. Various carbohydrates are known as cane or beet sugar, glucose, fructose, starch and cellulose. Starch and sugars are easily digested and have a high feed value, but cellulose, which forms a large proportion of the horse's natural feed, is digested only through the bacterial action which occurs in the caecum and large intestine. This accounts for the great size of these organs. In the process of digestion, carbohydrates are broken down into the simplest form and then absorbed through the wall of the gut into the bloodstream. They are used by the body as fuel for energy or stored, in the form of glycogen or fat, under the skin or in the liver and other internal organs.

Not only is fat formed in the body from carbohydrate and protein, but additionally from fat and oils which are eaten and digested, then absorbed into the body. Fat is a much more concentrated source of energy than carbohydrate, supplying about two-and-a-half times as much energy per pound.

Vitamins are special substances which are required in the diet in extremely small amounts in order to maintain life and health. Since their discovery early this century, a great deal has been learned about vitamins and the diseases that result in humans if they are not fed in sufficient quantities in the diet. For example, beri-beri results from a deficiency of Vitamin B, scurvy from Vitamin C deficiency and rickets from Vitamin D deficiency.

In practice, an absolute deficiency of these substances in the diet of a horse is unlikely. How much a partial deficiency can interfere with growth or with performance for work or for breeding is not known.

Minerals are necessary for the health of animals, and the importance of feeding common salt or calcium and phosphorus to livestock has been recognised for many years.

In addition, it is known that certain elements such as iodine, cobalt and copper are required in very small amounts (so small, it is usual to refer to them as 'trace' elements). Minerals have many vital functions in the body. The skeleton is composed almost entirely of the minerals calcium and phosphorus. Minerals are also necessary in the construction of the soft tissues.

Many people with a lifelong experience of feeding horses hold that good hay and oats are all that the stabled horse requires in the way of fodder. But opposing views are held that compound mixtures, together with various vitamin and mineral supplements, are essential for a correct diet. The latter approach, 'scientific feeding', aims to provide the 'exact' requirements for the various nutritional substances (vitamins, proteins, carbohydrates, etc) to maintain health and performance in the horse.

The two approaches have the same object, but in the first it is assumed that hay and oats, being a natural feed of horses, can supply all the necessary requirements without having to define them in exact terms. Those who feed along scientific lines maintain that this is an extremely erroneous assumption. They claim that good hay is very difficult to obtain or is virtually non-existent in this country because of bad summers, modern methods of baling, and the fact that the crop offers a relatively poor return to the farmers who grow it. The present day trend of feeding supplements of vitamins, minerals, dried milk and other concentrated foods is a direct result of the poor quality of hay which, more often than not, falls far short of many of the minimum nutritional levels required by the horse. If we knew the exact requirements of the horse at all stages of its life, it would indeed be logical to put these into a mixture and compound them into pellets or nuts, so as to avoid the feeding of an unbalanced or deficient diet. Another advantage of nuts is that a wide range of suitable grains and mineral supplements can be included in addition to hay and oats.

Unfortunately, very little is known about the exact needs of the horse for particular nutritional substances. The market for horse feeds is small compared with that for pigs and cattle. So manufacturers have little incentive to research the nutritional requirements of the horse.

It is also a much easier task to measure the efficiency of a diet if there is a definable criterion by which success can be measured.

In pigs, for instance, the efficiency of a particular diet or food can be assessed by weighing the pig at frequent intervals. It is very much more difficult to observe the effect of feeding on a horse's growth and performance when so many other variable factors are involved.

So what advice should the thoroughbred owner follow?

In a field where too little is known, it is probably better to build the diet on general principles rather than be too concerned with details. There are two questions of fundamental importance which the aspiring equine dietician should ponder before deciding on the horse's diet. What is the purpose for which the horse is kept? And does the horse have access to pasture or is it entirely stable fed?

In answer to the first question, we can distinguish two main purposes for which horses are kept and fed for growth, and for performance or work. As each purpose requires a somewhat different emphasis on quality or composition, and also quantity of food, the various categories involved must be recognised.

The growing horse includes the suckled foal, the weaned foal, the yearling, the two- and three-year-old and, to a lesser extent, the four-year-old. The last four months of pregnancy are also a most important growth period for the foetus and the pregnant mare therefore requires special attention at this time. In addition, mares kept for breeding require different types of diets, according to whether they are being mated, in the early stages of pregnancy, or suckling a foal.

Performance, or work, covers a multitude of different purposes, such as racing, hunting, riding or jumping. In each individual, the amount of energy expended depends on the stage of training or the severity of the work performed at any given time. The quantity of food required to meet these demands will vary accordingly. Yearlings, and two- and three-year-olds, fall into both groups and their diet must be adjusted to meet the demands of growth as well as that of performance. A further example of dual need is found in pregnant mares, who may be required to suckle their foal at the same time as nourishing a foetus developing within their uterus.

In general, the energy required for work or performance comes from carbohydrates, as provided by oats, whereas growing animals need a higher proportion of protein to satisfy the demand for growing tissues such as muscle. Protein is found in good hay made under ideal conditions. It may be deficient in a diet composed only of hay and oats, where the hay is sub-standard. However, before rushing to feed extra protein the implications of the second question should be considered; is the horse entirely stable fed or does it have access to pasture? Grass is the most natural of all horse foods, but it varies enormously in content at different times of the year. For example, the percentage of protein is very high in spring and summer grass, but low in winter. There is therefore a danger of over-feeding protein if stock is allowed to graze spring grass at the same time receiving stable feed containing a high proportion of protein. The opposite may occur in winter if the deficiency of protein in the grass is not made up by feeding a higher proportion in stable feed. Too much protein fed to young stock may lead to bony abnormalities, while too little will result in stunted growth, death of the foetus in the first two months of pregnancy, or foals that are weak at birth.

Protein is by no means the only constituent of the diet which needs to be fed in the correct proportions. For instance, the ration should contain roughly equal proportions of the minerals calcium, contained in hay (especially lucerne), and phosphorus of which bran has a high content. Bone is composed largely of these two minerals, so it is obviously very important, especially for growing animals, to see that they are present in the correct proportion.

When selecting a proprietary mineral supplement, it is important to realise that a horse in training, receiving hay and bran, will probably require more calcium than phosphorus to maintain a ratio of 1:1, whereas the yearling at stud, being fed on winter grass, may need equal quantities, as is found in bone meal.

As weaning time approaches, it must be remembered that the milk which the foal is receiving from its mother will contain an ideal proportion of calcium and phosphorus, as well as being a natural source of many other nutritive substances. This source is suddenly removed on the day of weaning and some effort must be made to compensate the newly weaned foal by adding dried skimmed milk or some other high-quality food to the staple concentrate ration.

It is comparatively easy for anyone who is responsible for the feeding of horses to obtain professional advice on the subject, whether from a vet or from a member of a nutritional advisory service.

29: Various types of colic

Colic is a word used in medicine to describe pain arising from any of the tubes of the body. These tubes include the bile duct and the ducts leading from the kidneys, as well as the gut itself. In the horse, colic is a term usually confined to pain arising from the gut or, as it is otherwise known, the alimentary canal (being the tube which runs from the mouth to the anus and along which food passes by a process of muscular contractions of the wall of the tube). These contractions, known as peristalsis, occur in waves and propel the contents on their way. As the food passes along the tube it is subjected to different processes to break it down so that the constituent substances can be absorbed through the bowel wall into the bloodstream. These processes are known as digestion which, in the horse, is largely carried out by bacteria. These micro-organisms break down the fibre and cellulose in the food and, in so doing, liberate the products useful to the horse.

The tube is not of the same diameter from one end to the other, but is divided into portions of different calibre depending on the function which they perform in digestion. Thus, the gullet or oesophagus is narrow, but very muscular and capable of quite considerable dilatation. Its function is merely to pass the food from the throat to the stomach. Digestion starts in the stomach, continues in the small intestine and from there into the caecum and large colon. It is in the last two portions of the tube that the bacterial digestion occurs and these organs are relatively enormous, occupying most of the abdominal cavity. The large colon is followed by the small colon which, as the name implies, is of much smaller diameter. It leads to the rectum and outside.

When any condition arises which prevents the normal passage of food along the tube, it is likely to cause pain through the stretching or irritation of the wall. When a horse feels pain in any part of its body, it will react to it in a characteristic way. For instance, if it feels pain in one of its limbs, it will show lameness. When the pain arises from the gut, it will adopt characteristic attitudes. These signs are very important to vets in the diagnosis of colic.

Unlike a doctor who can put questions to his human patient, the vet has to rely on the signs that he observes. If the pain is dull and not very severe, the horse will be correspondingly quiet, lie down a lot, look round at its flanks, and give the appearance of being uncomfortable. If the pain is more severe, the horse may stand and kick at its belly or get down and roll quite violently. When severe pain is present, the horse often lies on its back for long periods as if it gets some relief from so doing. When a horse is in great pain, it often breaks out in profuse or patchy sweating, although these signs vary with the individual since some horses naturally sweat more freely than others.

In almost all cases of colic the horse will stop eating and, depending on the type of colic, it may drink very little or a great deal. Sometimes it will merely put its muzzle into the water and swill its mouth through as if wanting to drink, without being able to do so.

Many cases of colic are caused by obstruction in part of the bowel. This may occur at any point along the tube. However, there are certain places where a simple stoppage is more likely to occur than others. For instance, the large colon turns on itself several times, so there are 'corners' where dry material is more likely to become lodged. Enormous quantities of dry matter may accumulate at these points and this produces a dull pain which may persist over a period of many days before treatment can clear it. At other parts, where the tube is relatively small in diameter (such as where the small intestines open into the caecum), a small amount of dry matter may lodge, causing obstruction.

Obstructions, however, are not all straightforward collections of matter within the lumen of the tube. There are conditions where a portion of the bowel may become paralysed for a time so that food will not pass through it. When a portion of the bowel wall becomes inflamed the whole gut may cease to move, as if in sympathy with the affected piece. The cause of this damage to the wall may be the result of the formation of a blood clot in the arteries supplying a very small portion of the gut, so cutting off its blood supply. This often follows where gut parasites have damaged the wall of the arteries in their migration along these vessels. Further complications arise when this inflammation affects the outer surface of the gut wall. The surface becomes 'sticky' and another loop of bowel may become attached to it so that adhesions form between the two.

A dramatic form of obstruction is seen when a length of gut becomes twisted. In this case, the obstruction is complete and nothing can pass. Unless relieved by surgical means, the animal dies within hours, suffering acute agony.

Whatever the reason for an obstruction, however small, in any part of the bowel, there is a tendency for the whole bowel to become inactive and for peristaltic movements to cease. Once the bowel is upset in this way and material is not passing through as quickly as it should, gas is likely to form, causing acute pain. This collection of gas is referred to as tympany. Because the horse digests by bacterial fermentation, the likelihood of gas forming in the bowel is very much increased. It is possible to hear the sounds made by the peristaltic movements by listening by ear or with a stethoscope on the flanks. This gives a valuable clue as to the condition. Another helpful method that veterinary surgeons use to diagnose what is happening within an animal is rectal examination. By passing an arm into the rectum, it is possible to feel through its wall to determine whether there are large masses of material present in other parts of the bowel and also whether there is a great amount of gas present.

The general state of the animal's condition can be gauged by the pulse and the membranes of the eye. Examination of the blood is also helpful for assessing the effect that the colic is having on the fluid balance of the body. The bowel is very much concerned with regulating the amount of fluid necessary to the life of the cells. Any bowel disturbance is likely to upset this balance. In addition to fluids, the levels in the body of substances such as sodium, potassium and bicarbonate, which are collectively known as electrolytes, all depend to a great extent on the proper functioning of the bowel.

Besides obstruction, colic can also be caused by over-activity in part of the bowel or too much fermentation of its contents. In these cases there is likely to be a great deal of tympany and also loose dungs or diarrhoea.

In diagnosing a case of colic, it is important to consider the type of dungs that are being passed. In the early stages, however, it has to be remembered that there may be normal dungs present in the rectum and these are passed first. Even if there is a stoppage, normal-looking dungs can therefore be passed for some time, but eventually hard, pellet-like faeces will appear from the seat of the stoppage. These are often coated with mucus which may be mistaken for worms. It is important to keep the dungs passed prior to the vet's arrival, while the colic lasts, for him to examine.

Having made a diagnosis as to the type of colic with which he is dealing, the vet can apply treatment. In general, this consists of keeping the animal out of pain. Nowadays there is a wide range of drugs which will do this and at the same time reduce the spasm of the muscle of the bowel wall, which occurs when it is stretched or irritated. Various laxatives, such as liquid paraffin, are given by stomach tube in order to lubricate the bowel, in addition to drugs which stimulate peristalsis, if such is necessary. If the fluid balance of the body is upset, this may be corrected in some measure by introducing the appropriate fluids and electrolytes into the bloodstream.

A horse that shows signs of colic should be kept in as big a box as possible, with plenty of straw for bedding. It is necessary to keep a constant watch and to reduce as much as possible the risks of the horse damaging himself. This can be done by rearranging the bedding and seeing that the horse does not become cast against the wall. Further, the vet should be advised if the horse rolls violently so that he can take measures to sedate the horse as necessary. People often think that they should keep a horse standing in the belief that if he rolls it will cause a twisted gut. There is no proof of this and it is more likely that the twist comes first and the rolling afterwards.

Some cases of colic can be prevented by avoiding irregular feeding habits, such as eating straw or the feeding of very dry feed on a restricted water intake. This, however, only applies to simple stoppages. Strict parasite control during early life will avoid damage to the blood vessels leading to colic caused by the young forms of red worm migrating in the blood vessels.

Most types of colic are followed by recovery, although, as noted, this is not so in the case of a twisted gut. Fatal results may also follow if the bowel wall becomes so stretched by gas that it ruptures. Rupture may also occur if the blood supply to a portion of the wall is cut off to the extent that death of that portion occurs. The contents of the gut then pass into the peritoneal cavity, setting up an acute and fatal peritonitis.

Grass sickness

Grass sickness is a misnomer. Horses can become affected by this fatal disease when their diet consists only of stable feed, including no grass at all. It is another example of a disease which has been given a traditional name, which has stuck even though it is misleading. It was originally thought that the disease was in some way caused by grass on account of the fact that most cases occur when horses are turned out to pasture in the spring and summer months.

Grass sickness has been well known in Scotland ever since the first recorded cases appeared in a military training camp near Dundee in 1911. From that time many more have occurred each year, either singly or in epidemic form. While the disease is largely confined to Scotland and the north of England (beyond a line from Morecambe Bay to Flamborough Head), cases have been reported in horse centres such as Newmarket and as far south as Hampshire.

Grass sickness shows itself in a number of different forms. The first symptoms, seen in the acute type, consist of difficulties in swallowing, so that water and food comes down the nostrils when the horse attempts to drink or eat. If the horse happens to have been eating grass, the discharge will probably be green in colour. The food is chewed very slowly and deliberately, and a great deal of saliva is produced which, due to the difficulty experienced in swallowing, drools out of the mouth and nostrils, forming long, slimy strands. These symptoms are in some way similar to those shown by a horse that has an obstruction in its gullet, such as may result from swallowing a piece of wood. If the horse has grass sickness, however, other signs soon appear: a general apathy and dejection (even sleepiness), trembling movements over the shoulders and flanks, and periodic patchy sweating, perhaps forming a foamy mass under the tail.

Many of the symptoms seen in a horse suffering from the disease have a striking resemblance to conditions descriptive of colic. This is unsurprising, in view of the fact that the gut becomes completely inactive, so that large amounts of foodstuff accumulate in the colon. These can be felt by the vet when he makes a rectal examination. These rock-hard formations in the gut may be mistaken at first for an ordinary stoppage or impaction, but in grass sickness the symptoms of distress and pain, which are unrelieved by any form of treatment, together with the difficulty in swallowing and salivation, soon distinguish the two conditions: the one simple and responding to treatment, the other incurable and leading to death within 24 or 48 hours. The stomach, which is relatively small in the horse, becomes enormously distended with fluid, so full in fact that the horse may actually vomit (a very rare occurrence in horses) and an evil smelling fluid will be seen issuing from its nostrils.

Clinicians who have had a wide experience in the condition comment that it is rare for the stomach to rupture, despite the great distension, in contrast to the ruptures that occur in colics when the stomach becomes full of gas. The paralysis of the bowel causes increasing pain and discomfort and profound disturbances in the fluid and salts balance of the body. The blood becomes more and more concentrated, and eventually the animal dies as a result of the toxic effects.

Unfortunately, at present there is no known cure. Temporary relief may be given by emptying the stomach of its contents through a tube passed down the gullet, injections of pain-killing drugs, and intravenous infusions. But these measures are entirely temporary, as the stomach refills with fluid and the effects of the drugs and transfusions quickly wear off.

In the simple types of colic, such as when a stoppage occurs, various drugs are given which stimulate the movement of the bowel, so that the usual processes of digestion are thereby restored. In marked contrast, in genuine cases of grass sickness, these drugs fail to produce the least activity of the gut even when they are given in large doses. In addition, the effect of treating a case of grass sickness with the traditional methods of administering liquid paraffin and other medicaments through a stomach tube, adds to the already over-distended stomach and makes matters worse rather than better.

Other forms of the disease include those that are so acute that the horse dies within a matter of hours. In more chronic forms, the victims may linger on for weeks and weeks, the flesh falling away until they resemble a living skeleton. In these, diarrhoea rather than constipation may occur and the symptoms of pain and difficulty in swallowing are usually much less pronounced or even absent, compared with the acute form. The abdomen becomes boarded and tucked up like a greyhound. Even in the chronic forms, complete recovery is very rare and the horses are usually of little further use once they have been affected.

Diagnosis of the condition is made from the symptoms, which are well recognised by most people in the areas where the disease commonly occurs, although somewhat perplexing to those who have never previously seen the condition. Research workers strongly suspect that grass sickness is a viral disease, but this has not as yet been proved. The main effects are on the nervous system and especially that part which controls the movement of the bowel. In recent years, workers in Sweden and at the Animal Health Trust at Newmarket have shown that important changes occur in some of the nerve cells which, in many respects, are not unlike those found in poliomyelitis, a viral disease of humans. There are other similarities which are worth noting, such as the way the disease appears sporadically or in epidemic form among a community of horses, sometimes seen year after year and then disappearing for long periods in a particular geographical locality. Of course, the similarities end there, and grass sickness has no direct connection whatsoever with poliomyelitis. Only horses suffer from the disease, to which all breeds and ages, irrespective of sex, seem to be equally susceptible.

During the 1920s when there was a very large working horse population in Scotland, a great deal of effort and money was spent in researching the problem. All sorts of grasses were tested and even the part played by insects was investigated, a great number being trapped and fed to horses for the purpose, but without success. Bacterial toxins, poisonous plants, mineral deficiencies and allergies, all have been investigated and found not guilty - or at least, not proven! As noted, it now seems most likely that the condition is caused by a virus.

Since it is a disease of some consequence, causing loss among ponies, hunters, and brood mares in many parts of the country, renewed research, using modern methods of virus investigation, might well be a worthwhile area of study for a research body. If a virus is in fact the cause and it were to be isolated, it might be possible to produce a vaccine. At the present time, inoculation against the disease is impossible and measures to prevent its occurrence are of little use. A susceptible horse, entering a grass sickness area, may succumb, while its resident companions escape, but there is no definite pattern to the way in which the disease appears, so it is virtually impossible to take avoiding action.

30: Heart and circulation

Everyone is familiar with the stethoscope, and it might almost be regarded as the badge of office of the medical or veterinary practitioner. In fact, the stethoscope is merely a simple instrument for listening to any sounds that may be produced within the body. In practice, sounds from the heart, lungs and intestines are of most help in diagnosis.

As long ago as 400 BC, Hippocrates wrote of the practice of listening to sounds within the body by applying the ear to the chest. Credit for the invention of the stethoscope, however, goes to a Frenchman, René Laennec, who was born towards the end of the 18th century. He applied his ear to the end of a roll of paper and was 'surprised and pleased to hear the beating of the heart much more clearly than if I had applied my ear directly to the chest'. Although we accept the stethoscope as a commonplace instrument today, at the time of its introduction to medical practice it was an object of ridicule and scorn in certain sections of the medical profession!

Modern electronics now make possible more advanced instruments which can be used both for listening to and recording the heart sounds. The production of a record of a beating heart enables the practitioner to listen to the heart sounds at leisure and within the laboratory long after the patient has departed. Further, the sounds can be recorded on paper as tracings, as in an electrocardiogram. Such tracings, known as a phonocardiogram, help distinguish sounds which otherwise might not be detected by the unaided ear.

Whatever methods are used to listen to the sounds within the body, it is always the interpretation of the significance of such sounds that is most important to doctor or vet. What can be gained from the study of the heart sounds of the horse? In the first place, it is necessary to understand just why the heart makes any noise at all while it is beating.

The heart acts as a pump which drives the blood of the body through two great circuits, one to the lungs and the other to the rest of the body. The sounds arise from the working parts of the pump, together with the noise that the flow of blood makes as it passes through. It should be appreciated that any fluid which flows through a pipe is liable to give rise to sounds, especially if the flow is rapid and parts of the wall project into the main flow. Under such conditions the flow, instead of being smooth, may be turbulent, forming eddies which give rise to the vibrations registered as sounds.

The heart of the adult horse normally beats 30-40 times a minute while the animal is at rest. Each beat represents one complete stroke of the pump, and while it is not possible to interpret every sound made during that time, there are a number of characteristic ones which can be identified as arising from particular structures or occurrences in the heart as it functions.

If reference is made to the diagram (Fig 30.1), it can be seen that the heart is divided into two sides, the left and the right. These two sides do not normally communicate with each other and each is divided into a first and second chamber called the atrium and the ventricle respectively. The walls of the chambers are formed of muscle, which is more abundant in the second chamber than the first. There is also a difference in the thickness of the wall of the left and right ventricles. The wall of the left ventricle is very much thicker than that of the right and this reflects the greater amount of work it has to do, as will be explained on page 128.

Just as any pump must have valves so that the fluid or air it is driving passes in one direction only, so the heart has its valves arranged in such a way that the blood passes through it from the veins into the arteries. The main driving power of the heart comes from the two second chambers (the right and left ventricles) and sets of valves are found at the entrance and exit of both of these chambers. The two sets of valves found between the first and second chambers are shown in the diagram. Those at the exit of the left ventricle (second chamber) are called the aortic valves, while those between the right ventricle (second chamber) and the artery to the lungs, are called the pulmonary valves (Fig 30.1).

Heart and circulation

The sounds heard when listening to the heart are made by the various structures while they are performing their function as a pump. As noted, these functions are to pump blood through both sides of the heart in two separate streams. The blood enters the chambers of the heart from the veins, as their walls relax, and is then forced by the second chamber into the arteries. The right side of the heart pumps the blood into the artery leading to the lungs, while the left side is responsible for maintaining the circulation to the head, body and limbs. The work of the left half of the heart is therefore greater than that of the right and it is for this reason that the walls of the second chamber on the left side are very much thicker and more powerful than those on the right.

After the blood has passed through the lungs, it returns in the veins to the left side of the heart, bringing with it the oxygen-rich blood for circulation to the organs of the body. This blood returns in the veins to the right side and so to the lungs. In this way, the blood in circulation passes through the two circuits arranged as a figure of eight.

While each part of the heart may make a sound, we are only able to distinguish a limited number by ear alone, even with the help of a stethoscope. Electronic instruments are more precise but, of course, there is no advantage in hearing sounds if they cannot be interpreted. By interpretation is meant the ability to say what structure is causing the sound as it is carrying out its particular function. For instance, when a valve closes it may make a characteristic noise. Of course, the veterinary surgeon is interested in deducing further, from the sound, whether the valve is functioning properly and efficiently.

Normally, each heartbeat represents a complete stroke of the pump. That is, a complete contraction of the heart muscle followed by a complete relaxation, during which time the chambers of the heart alternately empty and fill with blood. The sequence of events of the working parts of the heart is normally the same in each beat. Thus, a wave of contraction of the muscle passes over the first chambers and then the second chambers. In this way blood is propelled from one end to the other. As the second chambers are filling with blood, the valves at their entrance are relaxed, but when they are contracting and squeezing the blood into the arteries, these valves become shut, so preventing a backward flow into the first chamber. At this time, the valves open at the outlet of the second chamber to allow the blood to be squeezed past them into the arteries. When all the blood has been squeezed from the second chamber past these valves, they shut, so that blood does not return from the arteries. When blood is pumped from the heart, the pressure in the arteries rises and it is this pressure which propels the blood away from the heart along the arteries, whose walls are very elastic.

It should not be imagined that the opening and closing of the valves is an active process controlled by muscles. Rather, it is the result of difference of pressure in the flow of blood acting on the valves and causing them to function as they do. The edges of the valves float in the bloodstream, but they are attached in such a way

Heart and circulation

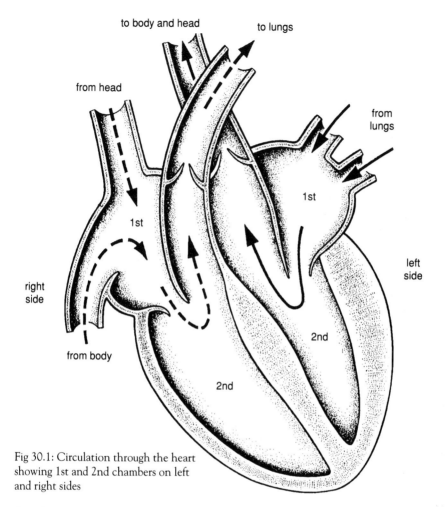

to body and head

to lungs

from head

from lungs

from body

right side

left side

1st

1st

2nd

2nd

Fig 30.1: Circulation through the heart
showing 1st and 2nd chambers on left
and right sides

that they open and close at the correct time, so preventing blood at all times from passing backwards against the main stream.

In the normal heart, there is an orderly sequence of events from which it is possible to interpret two sounds, called the first and second heart sounds. The first sound is associated with the contraction of the muscle of the first chambers and the opening of the first set of valves. The second sound is heard at the time the second set of valves, which are at the exit of the second chamber and the beginning of the arteries, close with a 'bang'. These two heart sounds are often called 'lubb dup', illustrating the rather slurred character of the first sound and the sharp character of the second.

Knowledge of which structures of the heart are associated with which particular sounds has come largely from experiments using catheters and other scientific methods. Some of the earliest experiments were, in fact, carried out on horses by a veterinary surgeon, Auguste Chauveau, in the latter half of the 19th century.

Fluid itself can cause sounds, especially when it is travelling fast through pipes or chambers whose walls are not completely smooth and when there are projections into the stream of flow. It is not surprising, therefore, that in the horse's heart conditions are set up whereby the flow is turbulent and eddies are formed, all of which may give rise to the vibrations which we hear as sound.

Murmurs

Such sounds made by the flow of blood are usually termed 'murmurs'. Again, it is possible to detect murmurs with the naked ear or with the aid of a stethoscope, and also with electronic instruments.

And again, it is the interpretation of murmurs with which the clinician is largely concerned. As the blood is forced through the heart on its way from the veins to the arteries, it passes through apertures of varying sizes under considerable pressure and with great speed. It is quite possible, therefore, that murmurs will be heard merely as a result of the conditions under which the blood is being driven through the heart, and not related to any damaged structure. In other words, a murmur does not necessarily mean that some structure is at fault within the heart, or even less that the efficiency of the heart is impaired. Murmurs can readily be detected with the stethoscope in many horses, some putting the figure as high as 70 per cent.

Given that by no means all murmurs are significant with regard to the proper functioning of the heart, the problem of interpretation is of supreme importance to vet and client. The evil reputation that murmurs have gained in the mind of the lay public arises, of course, from the fact that some murmurs are due to damaged valves. In such cases, the valve does not function properly and may, therefore, allow blood to escape in a backwards direction against the main flow. The turbulence that is set up gives rise to the sounds that we hear as murmurs. In these cases, the heart may not be fully efficient as a pump. Every pump needs power to drive it, whether it is the human arm, as in the case of a bicycle pump, or muscle, as in the case of the heart. If the valves are not fully efficient, the output of the pump can, to a certain extent, be maintained merely by increasing the driving power. At some point, however, the degree of inefficiency of the valves becomes so great that however much effort is put into the pump, the output will be adversely affected.

There are many questions involved in interpretation. Does the murmur arise as the result of blood flowing rapidly, but in a normal manner, through normal apertures and structures in the heart? In such a case, it is a normal heart functioning normally. Does the murmur come from damaged structures in the heart, and especially a damaged valve? If so, which valve is damaged and is the degree of

Heart and circulation

inefficiency likely to affect the horse when called upon to do extreme work? It should be remembered that the work demanded of a heart at rest is much less than that required during exercise.

The horse owner is mainly concerned with the amount of limitation that a damaged heart will impose on racing performance. Horses that perform badly on a racecourse (if they are not suspected of having been doped) are more often than not suspected of having heart trouble. Listening to the horse's heart with a stethoscope while it is in the stable is very helpful in confirming or allaying any suspicion. Such an examination can ascertain whether the heart is beating at the normal rate and rhythm. It is possible to hear if the heart sounds which are associated with the contraction of the heart muscle and the opening and closing of the valves are occurring in a normal sequence and so forth. It is also possible to hear if there are any murmurs and at what position over the heart area they are heard with the greatest clarity. For instance, a murmur heard more easily on the right side of the chest is most likely to be associated with the valves between the first and second chamber on the right side, while those heard best on the left side would indicate that their origins are structures on the left side of the heart. The position in which the murmur occurs relative to the normal heart sound - that is the first and second sound - is an additional clue to the site of origin of the murmur, since it is known at what stage of the heart beat these two sounds occur.

Listening to the sounds made during the heartbeat is a valuable aid to the veterinary surgeon seeking the state of health of a horse's heart but of course, as with any other examination of a medical nature, it is usually not enough to base conclusions on the evidence supplied by one type of investigation only. As far as the horse's heart is concerned, it is not possible unfortunately, to look at the heart itself as can be done in the human subject using radiography (X-ray). The horse's chest is much too large to make that a practical procedure. Nor has a convenient method yet been devised for testing blood pressure, which is a helpful adjunct to an examination of the heart in the case of humans.

Electrocardiogram

It is now over 80 years since Einthoven devised a machine for recording the electric current which passes through a heart when it is beating. Since that time it has become an established part of the examination of the heart by human cardiologists. The accumulation of knowledge derived from examinations by this technique in human subjects is, of course, immense. Although progress has been made in recent years on racehorses, much work still needs to be done before the full potential of this particular examination is fulfilled.

The electrocardiogram is the tracing or record of the current which passes in the heart muscle during the time it is beating. This current passes in a definite and particular path during each heartbeat. It follows the same course as the wave of muscular contraction as it passes over the walls of the first chambers and then over the second chambers. As the muscle relaxes, a further electrical disturbance is produced as the muscle returns to the resting state.

The instrument known as the electrocardiograph is capable of recording this electrical current or disturbance from electrodes placed on the surface of the body, usually on the limbs and the chest. The electrocardiogram only registers the passage of the electric impulse through the muscle and it has nothing to do with the valves or the flow of blood. As the electrocardiogram is the tracing of the impulse as it passes through the heart muscle, any damage in the muscle is likely to be reflected in changes of form in the tracing.

In addition, the tracing reflects the size of the various parts of the heart, especially the difference between the amount of muscle in the walls of the left ventricle and the right ventricle. When the right side of the heart comes under abnormal strain the difference in thickness of the walls between the two ventricles may be considerably less than normal, and this will be reflected in the tracing. If the heart is not beating in its normal rhythm, this may be the result of damage or interference in the special pathways which conduct the impulse through the heart. The electrocardiograph produces a written record indicating at what point this interference is taking place.

While electrocardiograms are not always easy to interpret (just as it is not always possible to interpret the heart sounds) it forms an important part of the examination of the horse's heart.

If a racehorse suffers from a virus infection, the heart muscle may be affected by an inflammation which is known as myocarditis. While a stethoscope cannot be expected to diagnose this type of injury to the heart muscle, the electrocardiogram is the preferred instrument in pursuit of this information. It is the writer's view that not nearly enough attention has been given in recent years to investigating this problem.

The heart muscle, as described, is the driving power of the pump and its well-being is of the greatest importance to the performance of the heart. If the work of the heart is increased, as in training, so the amount of heart muscle increases around both the second chambers of the heart. These two chambers, and especially the left one, are very intimately connected with the driving force of the heart and their walls become much thicker and more powerful as a result.

It is, of course, essential that the heart muscle receives an adequate oxygen supply because, if this organ fails, even temporarily through lack of oxygen the circulation will fail and the whole body will be affected. The supply of blood to the heart muscle comes from the arteries known as coronary arteries and not from the main flow of blood which passes through the heart chambers. If the flow of blood through these arteries is for any reason inadequate the heart muscle suffers, and this fact will often show in the electrocardiogram, although possibly only at times of exertion when the demand for oxygen is necessarily at its highest.

Heart and circulation

Echography (scanning) of the mare's ovaries and uterus are described on page 56. The technique is equally useful in assessing a horse's heart. By means of this instrumentation, it is possible to look into the heart and observe the valves in action. It is possible by such means to assess whether or not these organs are functioning properly.

It is also possible to determine the size of the various chambers and the thickness of their walls as blood is actually being pumped through the system. Further, the surface can be visualised to ascertain if there are any abnormal projections due to damage to the lining. This makes it possible to correlate murmurs with the action of the valves and other parts of the heart. The examination may include a modified type of ultrasound known as doppler. This enables the direction of blood flow through the heart to be observed to determine if it is normal. Doppler may be represented by colour so that it is possible to determine the presence of eddies or backflow on either side of the valves. For example, it may be that an affected valve causes blood to leak or spurt back through the valve abnormally. This would be heard as a murmur but now it can be seen through the doppler technique. Echocardiography and doppler present an enormous opportunity to evaluate a horse's heart.

However, the technique is limited compared to the use of such instrumentation in humans, largely because of the size of the patient and the way in which the heart lies in the chest. Ultrasound and doppler cannot pass through air and the horse's heart is partly covered by the lungs, which makes it difficult to see parts lying at the top (ie the base) of the heart.

Importance of blood tests

Blood plays a substantial part in every body function. Because of this, its composition to a large degree mirrors the state of health of the individual and is a source of useful information.

Blood is pumped away from the heart in tubes with thick muscular walls (arteries) to every part of the body. In the organs, these tubes divide into very fine tubes known as capillaries, and these pass into larger, thin-walled tubes, or veins, which carry blood back to the heart. In general, the greater the number of capillaries in any organ or part of the body, the greater is said to be the blood supply to that part.

The principal materials required by the living cell are sugar, amino acids, fats, vitamins, oxygen, salts and water. This applies to every cell of the body, whether it is a muscle fibre or the cell of one of the organs, such as the liver, kidney and so on. Blood forms a fully integrated and comprehensive transport system within the body, carrying all these vital substances from one point to another so that the cells' requirements are satisfied. It is blood that carries oxygen from the lungs to all the tissues of the body and returns with the carbon dioxide from the tissues to the lungs. It takes the products of digestion from the gut to the liver, and from the liver to all parts of the body. It collects the waste products from the cells and takes them to the kidney and to the gut so that they can be excreted from the body in the urine and the faeces.

Besides this tremendous task of transport carried out by the blood every minute of the day, the cells of the body must at all times be kept within the very narrow limits of a constant environment. If the change in concentration of the bloodstream of any of the vital substances is too marked, it will have a profound effect on the cells which the blood supplies. For instance, if the sugar content of the blood rises above or falls below the normal limits, as may happen in diabetic subjects, convulsions or coma may result. Insufficient oxygen results in serious brain damage, while marked variations in the content of such substances as sodium, potassium or calcium may cause heart failure or muscular spasms.

If blood is allowed to stand it separates out into two parts (Fig 30.2). The cells settle to the bottom, and above them will be seen a straw-coloured fluid (plasma) in which the cells are suspended. The cells of the blood are formed in the bone marrow and to a lesser extent in certain other organs.

The great majority of these cells are red blood cells and a much smaller percentage are white cells.

The red cells contain a pigment known as haemoglobin, which conveys the oxygen. The white cells play a part in the defence of the body. Blood also contains special white cells called platelets, which form part of the clotting mechanism. Protein, sugar and salts, enzymes, antibodies and hormones are found in the plasma. A large proportion (about 90 per cent) of plasma consists of water, which makes a major contribution to the fluid balance of the body.

The adult horse contains about 8 gallons of blood in its circulation, although this will vary considerably with the individual. The body also possesses a large reserve of blood in the spleen, which can be rapidly mobilised into the circulation in exercise or moments of stress.

In veterinary and medical practice, transferring relatively large quantities of blood from one individual to another is standard practice. By collecting the blood into a fluid which prevents clotting, it is possible to transfuse it back into a sick person or animal. Transfusion between horses is a simple procedure and there is less risk of the donor's blood being incompatible with that of the patient than there is in human medicine. However, tests should be performed before transfusion to ensure that the blood of the donor is compatible to that of the recipient. Blood transfusions may be given to restore the normal blood volume in cases of haemorrhage or shock following surgical operations, or to restore the number of circulating red cells if for any reason these are being destroyed, as they are in certain diseases. Transfusions are also useful for supplying antibodies, proteins and other substances from a healthy individual to a sick one.

By taking samples of blood and counting the number of cells or analysing the amount of different substances contained in a known quantity, it is possible to pursue

Heart and circulation

Fig 30.2: The separation of blood into cells (bottom) and straw-coloured plasma (top)

the diagnosis of illness beyond the limits of external examination. In the horse, knowledge of the normal values of the various constituents of the blood has still some way to go before full use can be made of blood examination. However, from an examination of the cells, it is possible accurately to assess whether or not a horse is anaemic (*ie* too few red cells or too little haemoglobin present in the blood).

The presence and to a lesser extent the nature of an infection, can be confirmed by the type and number of white cells which are found circulating in the blood. The estimation of certain salts, proteins and enzymes in the blood is valuable in the diagnosis of disease of the liver, muscle and kidneys. Antibodies circulating in the blood can be detected by laboratory methods, and information thereby obtained on certain important aspects of infectious disease. The proportion of cells to fluid of plasma in the blood gives an indication of the state of the fluid balance in the horse (*ie* whether or not the animal is in a dehydrated state).

Besides investigations into various diseases, research workers in many parts of the world have been assessing the results of certain blood tests against the ability or fitness of a horse to race. Modern laboratory techniques have made possible the

The lymphatics

measurement of an ever-increasing number of constituents of blood, with a corresponding increase in accuracy. However, these tests must be taken in the context of the whole patient. There is a growing and regrettable tendency for those dealing with performance horses to attempt to simplify answers, pinning a whole diagnosis as to whether, for example, an individual is suffering from a virus, on a single element of a blood test. In reality, each test on blood represents a part of a jigsaw puzzle. The results of a number of tests form only one part of the puzzle. The whole picture is based on all the parts including the clinical examination and physical tests related to performance. Similarly, it is becoming a habit to use blood tests to ascertain the fitness of a horse. However, these tests cannot be expected to replace conventional methods of training any more than they replace conventional methods of diagnosis and disease. Blood tests must be regarded as an aid to diagnosis and not a means of making the diagnosis itself.

31: The lymphatics

Most people have experienced a swollen gland in the neck or in the armpits at some time in life and many have probably felt similar enlargements in the throats of horses. These glands, or lymph nodes as they are sometimes called, are part of a network of vessels which, like the blood vessels, play an important transport role in the body. The vessels and their associated glands are called the lymphatic system. They consist of closed tubes which ramify over the entire body in a manner similar to the blood vessels with which they may be compared. Instead of containing blood, they contain a fluid called lymph.

The blood system consists of arteries, capillaries and veins, through which the blood is driven by the heart. Unlike the blood vessels, the lymph vessels do not form a complete circle, but begin in the extremities and organs as a network of capillaries with blind endings. These lymph capillaries, just like their counterparts, the blood capillaries, have very thin walls and they collect together to form larger vessels with thicker walls. The latter have valves which prevent the flow of lymph from passing in a backward direction towards the blind-ended capillaries.

Lymphatic vessels are present in all organs and tissues of the body with certain exceptions, such as the central nervous system. Eventually they collect into one duct which opens into the large veins close to the heart.

Before entering the bloodstream the lymph must pass through one or more lymph nodes. These nodes are present in enormous numbers in many different parts of the body, but only in certain circumstances, when they become enlarged, is their presence felt. Each part of the body possesses lymph capillaries which carry the lymph fluid away from that part, through a gland and then into the bloodstream. There is a continuous flow of lymph just as there is a flow of blood within the blood vessels but, as the vessels containing the lymph do not form a complete circle as is found in the blood vessels and as the lymph is not driven by a special organ such as the heart, it is not surprising to find that the mechanism of flow is somewhat different. The flow is maintained by the movement of the surrounding parts, such as muscles and tendons which massage the fluid along the vessels. Back-flow is prevented by valves, as noted. There are other complex physical factors which help maintain the flow of lymph, primarily within the internal organs such as the liver, kidneys and so on, where there is no muscular movement.

Lymph is continually being formed in the capillaries of the lymphatic system and passing from there to the central point of discharge, into the bloodstream. To understand the function of lymph and why it is necessary to have a kind of backdoor entrance to the bloodstream, the reader must be familiar with the terms 'tissue space' and 'tissue fluid'. All tissues are composed of cells and these cells are bathed in fluid which is found in the spaces around them. Tissue fluid acts as a kind of middle man between the bloodstream and the cells, bringing to the latter the nourishment they require and also providing them with the necessary salts and physical environment they need for existence. If, for instance, the tissue fluid becomes too concentrated, the cells shrink and eventually die. The arrangement of the blood and lymph capillaries and the tissue space is shown in Fig 31.1. One purpose of the lymph stream is to keep in balance the amount of salts and protein in the tissue spaces. There is a continuous flow of fluid from the bloodstream into the tissue space and then again into the lymph stream or back into the bloodstream, so that another of the functions of the lymphatics is to maintain a proper fluid balance.

Lymph is a colourless or yellowish fluid, which contains certain white corpuscles similar to those found in blood, salts and a small amount of protein. Most of the cells of the lymph are small, round cells called lymphocytes. The lymph nodes act as a kind of filter to the lymph stream as it passes through them. Any foreign particle in the lymph tends to become arrested in these glands. For instance, the carbon particles in the smoke inhaled by people who live in cities land on the lining of the air tubes in their lungs. They then enter the lymph stream which comes away from the lung and are taken up by the filter of the glands through which the lymph stream passes. These glands, therefore, are found at post mortem to be very black as they contain a great deal of carbon. In a similar way, bacteria may become arrested in the lymph nodes and unless the gland is able to kill them, they breed and cause a disease of the lymph node itself, as will be seen later. Tumour cells may also find their way into the lymph stream and spread through the body, affecting many of the lymph nodes.

In the horse we recognise many conditions and diseases which are associated with the lymphatic system. For instance, when a horse's legs are 'filled' and subsequently 'walk down', there is an over-filling of the tissue spaces with fluid, subsequently eliminated by speeding up the lymph flow by the muscular activity of exercise. Whether the legs fill because there is too much fluid leaving the blood vessels or too little entering the lymph stream is never certain, as the factors affecting the balance of the fluid are closely interrelated. One of the functions of the

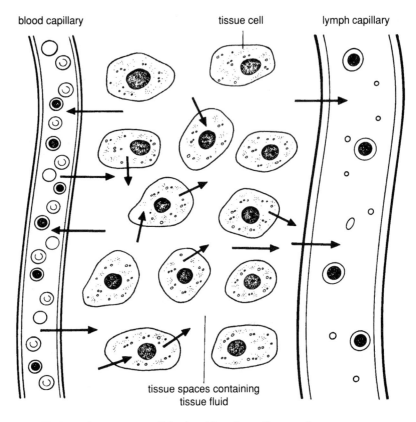

blood capillary   tissue cell   lymph capillary

tissue spaces containing
tissue fluid

Fig 31.1: Arrangement of blood and lymph capillaries and tissue spaces

lymph stream is to take away excess protein from the tissue fluid and, as any horseman will tell you, the legs tend to fill in a horse that has a rich diet and no exercise. Further, anything which interferes with the free flow of the lymph stream prevents the surplus fluid being carried away from the part. This may result from a tight bandage or injury to the lymph vessels so that they become blocked.

When the lymph vessels become inflamed - a condition known as lymphangitis - the surrounding area becomes enlarged, hot and painful to the touch. While this may occur in any part of the body, it is most commonly seen and talked of as lymphangitis when the limbs are involved, particularly the hind limbs. In this case, the lymphatic vessels become engorged with lymph and proper flow is prevented. Lymphangitis may be caused by any factor that prevents proper flow of lymph, but especially by infection. Bacteria entering through a cracked heel or infected wound in the lower part of the limb may enter the lymph stream and set up an infection in the gland and vessels through which the lymph passes on its way up the limb. Once

        The lymphatics

the glands and the vessels have been affected in this way, they are more susceptible to subsequent recurrences of the condition. In some cases, the disease may become chronic and a permanently enlarged leg result. The principal treatments of lymphangitis are the administration of appropriate antibiotics to help kill the bacteria, anti-inflammatory drugs to reduce the inflammation, and exercise to help restore the flow of lymph in the affected part.

Any poison, bacterial toxin or allergic reactions of the body to such things as drugs and foreign bodies tend to affect the walls of the blood and lymph capillaries. In this case they will allow fluid and other substances to pass through them in an abnormal manner. In this way, the fluid balance in the tissue spaces will be upset, and this is one reason why we get filled legs in horses in many differing illnesses.

There are three infectious diseases which primarily affect the lymphatic system. One of the most common and well-known in this country is strangles.

Strangles and glanders

Strangles is a highly infectious disease which affects horses of all ages. It is caused by bacteria, which are a type of streptococcus, but which are distinct from the ordinary streptococcus commonly found in the genital tract and other organs of the body. In the majority of cases the disease is seen in an acute form, the animal suffering from a high temperature, a watery discharge from the nostrils, turning thick and pus-like in nature, and swollen, painful lymph glands, especially those of the head and neck. Abscesses form in these lymph glands, and after a few days or weeks, burst to the outside through the skin, discharging a thick pus containing the causal germ.

The strangles bacteria enter the body by being inhaled, setting up a catarrhal condition of the mucous membranes lining the nasal passages. At the same time, however, the germ enters the lymphatic vessels which drain the lymph away from the mucous membranes and from there are carried to the neighbouring lymph glands. In these glands they breed, causing the abscesses mentioned.

Areas most commonly affected are those between the angle of the lower jaw and in the region of the pharynx. These can be seen as swellings in the area immediately below the base of the ears on either side. When the glands swell they are tender and for this reason may cause the animal difficulty in swallowing before they burst. In a small proportion of cases involved in an epidemic, other lymph nodes in the body may become affected and abscesses form in such areas as the groin or internally. The term 'bastard strangles' has been used to describe these particular cases.

Strangles is not usually a fatal disease, especially now that antibiotics are available for treatment. It can, however, cause serious complications. These result from the damage caused by the toxins liberated at the time of infection and which affect the nerves of the body, possibly resulting in the paralysis of the vocal cords, the soft palate, and so on. They may also seriously impair the function of the heart and lungs so that there is a permanent weakness in these organs.

The treatment of strangles consists of giving antibiotics to which the bacteria are sensitive. As they are killed by most antibiotics there is very little difficulty in this respect. Early diagnosis is important, not only so that treatment may be applied, but also to prevent the spread of the condition which, as noted, is highly infectious.

The symptoms may easily be confused with other infections which cause a heavy nasal discharge, with or without swellings in the lymph nodes. Most of the latter conditions, such as those caused by viruses followed by secondary bacterial infection, either do not cause the swelling of the lymph glands or do not have the high temperature rise which is nearly always seen in strangles. In order to make certain of a diagnosis, however, it is necessary to collect material from a burst abscess or from the nasal discharge and submit it to laboratory tests.

Like all other infectious diseases that occur on epidemic scale, the number of affected individuals in any community and the severity of the symptoms vary over the years. Two important factors involved in this changing pattern are the virulence of the infective organism concerned and also the degree of immunity within the individuals of the population. At the present time the amount of strangles in thoroughbreds in this country does not appear to be very great. However, from time to time, outbreaks do occur on the studs or in training stables. It is also fairly prevalent among ponies and riding horses.

In considering disease control and measures to prevent the spread of infections, strangles must always be included on the list. The same principles such as isolation and disinfection which apply to other infectious diseases are also recommended for this disease. The immunity of a population of horses against strangles can be raised effectively by vaccination. The efficacy of any particular vaccine will, however, vary according to the nature of the outbreak. There is also, as with other vaccines, the possibility of unpleasant reactions at the site of injection in some individuals. For this reason, and because the threat of strangles has not appeared to be of very widespread economic significance in recent years, vaccination in this country is not practised on a large scale.

It is quite common for horses, especially young ones, to develop abscesses in the lymph nodes under the jaw, which simulate strangles. These may contain many different bacteria but not the one causing strangles. From time to time, the appearance of these swellings is therefore mistaken for strangles, as occurred at a South Coast meeting. The ordinary streptococcus and the staphylococcus are associated with this benign type of abscess and occasionally an organism known as *Corynebacterium equi*. The latter germ may also be responsible for small, slow-growing abscesses in the lymph nodes in other parts of the body such as those draining the gut, but it is usually only recognised by the horse-owning community as a distinct disease when it causes pneumonia in foals. In this condition, abscesses form in the lymph nodes within the chest and amongst the lung tissue itself. The affected animals then show symptoms of respiratory trouble, including a discharge from the nostrils, coughing and an increased rate of breathing. The typical sounds of

The lymphatics

pneumonia can be heard through the stethoscope or by listening directly with the ear against the chest wall. There is a gradual loss of condition, together with periods of elevated temperature, which fluctuates between 102°F and 105°F. The condition does not respond to antibiotics and is generally fatal, after a prolonged course lasting several weeks. In Australia, this pneumonia may occur in epidemic form on some studs with a large number of foals affected. In England, cases usually occur singly, a stud maybe close-up experiencing only one over a period of years.

It is often difficult to distinguish between a pneumonia caused by other organisms and the *Corynebacterium*. At post mortem, the disease is easily identified by the large abscesses which are present in the lymph nodes and the lung tissue. These abscesses contain a thick yellowish-white pus, from which the bacteria are easily identified. Because the abscesses have thick walls, any antibiotic used in treatment has little chance of penetrating and killing the bacteria. This is the reason why there is not the response to treatment one would expect, even though very high doses of antibiotics are used.

One of the most serious diseases primarily associated with the lymphatic system is glanders. This disease has been seen in most countries, causing serious losses among horses. In addition, the glanders organism can also affect man with a fatal result. Britain has been free from the disease since 1928, but by law it is still a notifiable disease. This means that its control is in the hands of the local authorities and the Ministry of Agriculture, Fisheries and Food (MAFF) like such diseases as foot and mouth and anthrax.

Glanders may be an acute or chronic disease. In the chronic form, the disease usually has a slow and insidious onset with an occasional rise in temperature and perhaps a cough. Nodules appear in many parts of the body, including the mucous membranes, skin and internal organs, and these tend to break down to form ulcers. A pneumonia develops, together with symptoms of nasal catarrh. The latter becomes progressively more copious and the lining of the nasal passages increasingly reddened with nodules, with ulcers developing on the nasal septum. The lymph glands below the jaw become enlarged and often adhere to the bone and the skin so that they cannot be moved. These glands may eventually burst but are much slower to do so than the strangles abscess.

In the acute form of the disease the onset is more rapid, with an elevated temperature and the development of numerous nodules and ulcers in the lining of the nose over a period of two or three days. A profuse and blood-stained nasal discharge appears and large oedematous swellings occur in various parts of the body. The lymph glands become rapidly enlarged and may burst, while affected individuals become thin and their breathing laboured. The acute form of the disease usually ends fatally after a week or so.

Various tests, similar to those applied in tuberculosis, are used for diagnosis. The application of an extract of the bacillus, known as mallein, results in a typical reaction at the site of injection in those animals affected with glanders.

Regulations controlling the movement of horses into this country from abroad have resulted in the elimination and prevention of glanders during the last 60 years.

32: Nervous ailments

Some of the terms used by horsemen and vets alike are highly descriptive of the symptoms of equine ailments. Anyone who has seen a 'wobbler' would probably agree that the term is a vivid one. In this condition, the horse loses proper control of its hind limbs, so that in motion it sways or wobbles in an alarming fashion. In the early stages, when the condition is not very advanced, signs may only be apparent when the horse is trotted and brought to a sudden halt. The lack of control of the hindquarters is seen at that particular moment. Likewise, it may occur at the time of turning the horse in a tight circle or when it is made to take backward steps. As the condition progresses, the signs become more obvious and are even apparent at the walk.

Most people take the normal movements of the body for granted and it is only when disease sets in and there is interference with normal function that we marvel at the healthy state. In motion, this is even more apparent in a four-legged animal where the movements of the limbs are wonderfully co-ordinated. It is only when one limb or more fails to function properly for any reason that particular interest is taken in the horse's movements. When the normal control of one or both of the hind limbs is interfered with, the abnormality in gait will not escape notice by even the most inexperienced observer. The loss of control may result in stumbling or knuckling over the hind fetlock joints and sometimes an exaggerated movement in the flexion of one or both of the hind limbs during walking and trotting. This latter action is often described as 'stringhalt' although it can frequently occur in horses which show no other signs of being wobblers.

While the term 'wobbler' cannot be improved upon to describe the symptoms, it tells nothing of the cause of the condition. The limbs are a system of struts and levers manipulated by the muscles which are bunched high up in the limbs and on the body. Muscles are controlled by nerves and it is interference with these nerves that results in the loss of control of the muscles and, therefore, the inco-ordination of the limb movements. The nervous system consists of the brain, the spinal cord and the nerves which leave the cord and run to and from the organs and muscles of the body (Fig 32.1). The whole can be likened to a telephone system where the exchange represents the brain, and the cables leaving the exchange the spinal cord, collected in one large group or column, from which the lines emerge to the individual houses. In this analogy, the houses are the muscles. Just as the telephone system relays messages, so the nerves convey information from various parts of the body and pass this information to the brain or automatically, on shorter paths, back to the muscles in such a way that they are caused to contract or relax according to the state of motion.

Damage at any point in this highly complex system is bound to upset the passage of messages to and from the muscles, so interfering with the co-ordinated movements and of the awareness of the animal of the whereabouts of its limbs.

Knowledge of the cause of wobblers is incomplete. It is probable that the symptoms shown may result from damage in the horse's nervous system at many different parts. Damage to the spinal cord, especially in the neck, will result in the symptoms of inco-ordination. The cord, in fact, runs through a canal in the vertebrae and in this way it is very well protected from injury. But damage here may be the result of a dislocation or partial fracture of the vertebrae, or from abscess formation and bony growth pressing on the cord. Any process which is likely to result in pressure within the bony canal has little outlet and the results are consequently more serious than if the cord were surrounded by soft tissue.

Symptoms of stringhalt, when the hind limbs flex sharply in movements which are not associated with wobbling, are also probably due to some damage or interference with the nerve pathways, although the exact nature of the condition is not known. Horses showing symptoms of stringhalt may go many years before they are in any way affected in their performance.

'Shivering' is another nervous ailment which may, or may not, be associated with stringhalt and wobbling. If the hind limb of a shiverer is flexed or maybe the foot hit with a hammer, tremors will be seen running over the tail and the hindquarters, and the horse returns its limb to the ground in a jerky or shaky manner.

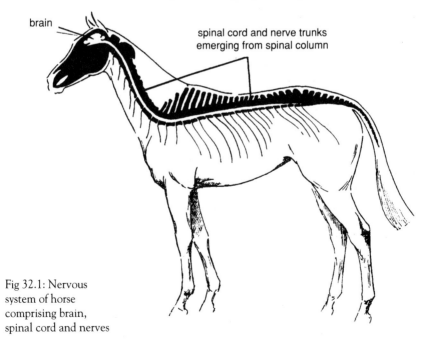

brain

spinal cord and nerve trunks emerging from spinal column

Fig 32.1: Nervous system of horse comprising brain, spinal cord and nerves

Nervous ailments

There are other nervous disorders about which little is known of the cause and which may be no more than habits. 'Crib biting', when the horse seizes hold of any convenient fitting in the stable such as the manger, arches it neck and swallows repeatedly, is a most annoying and unsightly stable vice. 'Windsucking' is a similar habit, although in this case the animal may perform it without necessarily taking hold of anything with its teeth. Although such habits are thought to arise from the fact that the animal is stabled for long periods, they may not always disappear when the horse is turned out and, in this case, it may use the rails of the paddock on which to bite. Crib biting can only be diagnosed by seeing the animal performing the act, but if the front teeth are examined and found to have severely worn edges, it is enough to arouse suspicion.

Another stable habit, or vice, is described as 'weaving'. This apt description applies to horses that weave their head and neck from one side to the other for long periods. This is usually done with the head held low to the stable door. If the movements are excessive and prolonged, as in some cases, damage may be caused to the tendons of the forelimbs from the continual strain of the shifting of weight from one limb to the other.

All such habits are usually classed as unsoundness, as they often lead to loss of body condition or even damage to vital structures, besides being unsightly in appearance.

33: Infectious diseases

Infection denotes the entry of harmful microbes into the body. The microbes may be bacteria, virus or fungus. Each category has its own characteristics.

Bacteria are germs that live among but not within body cells, causing their destruction. They attract the white blood cells known as neutrophils and hence the formation of pus which is largely composed of millions of white cells killed in the process of engulfing bacteria. Bacteria can be observed under the light microscope when suitably stained and they may be cultured on special plates of nutrient substances known as media. The bacteria grow in colonies on the surface of such plates (Fig 33.1).

Viruses are a thousand times smaller than bacteria and can be viewed only by electron microscopes. They live within the cells of the body and become incorporated in functional components of the cells. In many cases, they may actually take over the control of the cell for varying periods. Viruses reproduce within the cell and then break out when the cell dies, the liberated particles re-entering other cells to continue their life cycle.

Fungi are plant-like and consist of filaments known as hyphi. These produce spores which germinate into further hyphi and therefore represent the reproductive capacity of the fungus. Fungus can penetrate the body but is often to be found on the surface of the skin (ringworm) or on ulcerated or abraided surfaces such as the eye, placenta, guttural pouch (in association with nose bleeds) and in the gut (diarrhoea).

Fig 33.1: Cultures of bacteria can be studied in the laboratory

The symptoms of infection are due to a number of effects caused by the microbes. Some microbes release a poison (endotoxin) resulting in malaise and fever. Then there is the release of various substances as a result of damage to the cells and tissues infected by the microbes. Depending on the nature of the microbe and the reaction it causes in the body, symptoms of inflammation may be experienced in general or in local terms. An abscess in the foot or lower part of the limb, for example, causes heat, swelling and pain. The pain causes lameness which may be the first symptoms to be observed.

Infections of the liver, kidney, brain or lungs cause damage to those organs and symptoms are related to the disturbances they cause. For example, in the brain (meningitis) headaches and nervous disorders, in the lungs rapid and difficult breathing, in the kidneys depression as a result of toxic substances accumulating in the bloodstream instead of being filtered by the kidney.

Boils, abscesses, genital infections and such-like may be caused by any one of a number of microbes but there are a number of specific infections affecting horses. The following are some of the more common examples.

Strangles is a disease of horses caused by a microbe known as *Streptococcus equi*. This germ should not be confused with the more common *Streptococcus* that is ubiquitous and occurs in abscesses, genital infections or wherever damage is suffered to the tissues. *S equi* is inhaled or eaten and penetrates the nasal airways and pharynx. It then penetrates the lymphatic system where it causes abscesses in the lymph nodes that form part of that system. The symptoms of strangles are fever, nasal discharge and swollen painful glands, usually of the head and neck, *ie* between the lower jaws and in the area below the base of the ears. The condition is highly infectious and is passed readily from one individual to another largely by the germ being exhaled and then inhaled by a susceptible contact. It may also be picked up from contaminated water and food mangers and from pus and catarrh which has been deposited on fences or pasture. Vaccines are available but are not very effective. The condition is usually not fatal and follows a course of some days or weeks at the end of which the lymph node abscesses burst and discharge a yellowish, creamy pus.

Viral disease in horses has become almost synonomous with coughing in racehorses and abortion in mares. This is because coughing is a common symptom in racing stables and is generally associated with poor performance. 'The virus' is often offered by trainers and owners as an explanation of poor performance affecting stables in epidemic proportions. However, as with all medical and veterinary problems, the explanation is not always that simple. There are some conditions which can be ascribed to a single definite microbe such as influenza. But others are the result of a combination of differing microbes and differing environmental circumstances. In the case of stabled horses, it may be the combination of one of a number of viruses followed by infection of the airways with bacteria, the resulting bronchitis aggravated by dust and forced exercise.

Some viruses, such as the equine herpes virus (EHV) can be identified in veterinary laboratories but others are as yet unknown and unidentified. Herpes virus infections have been well researched because they cause not only respiratory disease but also, in a small proportion of cases, may cause a pregnant mare to abort. Herpes viruses are spread from affected individuals to others through air contaminated by breath, sneezing or coughing. Horses of all ages are susceptible but the younger they are, the more nasal discharge will occur. In older individuals infections may be symptomless. The herpes infection is therefore one cause of colds that may run through a yard of horses and be responsible for below average performance of affected individuals. The infection is usually followed by secondary infection with bacteria and it is these that are responsible for the catarrh.

Despite many years of research since the recognition of viral abortion in Lexington, USA, during the thirties, it is still not clear why this common infection of horses' airways occasionally causes abortion in pregnant mares. In many instances, such abortions occur singly but in others there are catastrophic epidemics so that up to 50 per cent of pregnant mares on an infected studfarm may abort. These abortion storms are fortunately not very common but one or more seems to occur each year.

There are a number of herpes viruses affecting horses. EHV1 causes colds and abortion whereas EHV4 causes cold and only very occasionally an abortion. EHV2 occurs commonly and is not thought in itself to cause disease but may have some association with EHV1 infection. EHV3 causes the spots or coital exanthema of the external genital organs of stallions and mares.

Infectious diseases

The influenza virus causes a very similar disease to that experienced by humans: high fever and a harsh hacking cough lasting several days, followed in a few cases by nasal catarrh but more often a complete recovery provided the patient takes bed rest. In the case of the horse, avoiding exercise for about ten days is important to avoid subsequent complications. There are two known strains of influenza virus affecting horses: A-equi I and A-equi 2. These are different from strains affecting other species such as man, where there are many more strains and a distinct tendency for strains to alter slightly over the years. These variations make vaccinations more complicated than in the horse, where only two strains apply.

Vaccination is largely successful in protecting individuals and in preventing epidemics spreading through the horse population. There are a number of vaccines available, for both strains of equine influenza virus. These have to be given once or twice each year to boost the immunity produced by two injections given about four weeks apart at the commencement of the individual's vaccination programme. Vaccination against influenza may not protect 100 per cent.

Control of infectious diseases

Prevention is better than cure, particularly in the case of infectious diseases. Everyone should be on guard against promoting the spread of infection. It is a duty to prevent, if at all possible, healthy individuals coming in contact directly or indirectly with unhealthy ones. This responsibility rests on observation and action. Any symptom suggestive of infection - including one or more of fever, discharge from any orifice (nostrils, eyes, ears, vagina), diarrhoea or coughing in any individual - should be a matter for concern. The more individuals that are showing the same symptoms, the greater the contagious infection present.

Action in such circumstances should include:

(1) Taking veterinary advice, at least to the extent of a phone call to discuss whether or not a visit is necessary. Infection may have to be diagnosed by veterinary examination coupled with tests to aid the diagnosis and to confirm its nature.

(2) Isolation, as far as possible, of the affected individual until such time as a diagnosis can be made, and of contact animals until they can be examined for evidence of spread of the infection.

(3) Rational measures which may help to avoid further spread such as restricting movement of animals within or between studfarms and stables. The Horserace Betting Levy Board issues an annual Code of Practice for the control of infectious diseases affecting breeding stock. Advice is given with respect to EHV1 infection, equine arteritis and contagious equine metritis.

(4) Vaccination where vaccines are available and are judged to be effective. At present, there are vaccines on the market in the UK against EHV1 and influenza. Vaccines against strangles are available but judged not to be particularly effective.

34: Parasites

Hot, sunny weather is unfortunately accompanied by flies, which, besides being a general nuisance, spread various diseases. They bring a lot of misery to horses and no one who has seen a horse with its face covered by flies can doubt that he would prefer a return to colder, windy days. Besides the common housefly, which breeds in manure and other refuse, there are a number of other types which cause harm to horses.

Two of these, the bot and the warble, are closely related. Both have no mouth parts and never feed, apparently living only in order to lay their eggs. From these eggs develop larvae or maggots which enter and live in animals for varying periods of time. They then emerge and hatch into the fly. The warble maggot is a common parasite of cattle. Most racing stables used to have one or two affected animals each year. However, the drug Ivermectin, in use over the past ten years has all but eliminated warble fly maggots.

The warble fly is just over half an inch long and its body is covered with yellow hair with a band of darker hairs round the middle of its abdomen. They are most active in the months of June and July, when they lay their eggs on the hairs of the limbs of animals. The young maggots or larvae hatch from the eggs and crawl down the hair to the skin which they penetrate. They wander about just below the skin growing in size as they make their journey, which lasts for many months. Towards the spring they eventually find their way to the back and by this time they measure about half an inch. They partially penetrate the skin, making a small hole under which they live for varying times (usually about 30 days). During this stage, they grow very rapidly to perhaps an inch or more. During April and May, the mature maggot wriggles out of its hole in the skin and falls to the ground. So, after about a year, the cycle is completed.

When the maggot is preparing to leave the horse it often causes a large swelling which may be hot and tender to the touch. In the centre of the swelling is the pin-sized hole made by the maggot. Thick tracts about the size of a finger may be seen running towards the swelling. While the maggot may leave at this time, it will sometimes travel to another point in the horse's body before emerging, thereby causing a second swelling. The maggot may die and be absorbed by the tissues, but it is nevertheless dangerous to squeeze the swellings so that the maggot is squashed. The result may be a tissue reaction which, in extreme cases, has been known to result in death of the horse.

Apart from the pain that the maggot causes, the introduction of local infection that follows their penetration of the skin leads to small boils. Many animals lose condition as the result of the wandering larvae and serious setbacks in training may result. When the saddle area is affected it may not be possible to ride the animals for several days. Treatment consists of local application of heat usually in the form of a poultice so as to encourage the maggot to come to the surface of the skin and leave the body.

As cattle are the only significant source of the parasite, the complete elimination of maggots from this species would also lead to its disappearance in horses.

The bot fly is brown and hairy, not unlike a bee. It is about the same size as the warble fly, but it occurs during late summer and lives only a few days. It usually lays its eggs, which are yellow in colour, on the hairs around the fetlocks and over the shoulder region, where they can easily be seen. The larvae hatch in about ten days and find their way to the mouth of the animal by being rubbed or licked. They wander about the cheeks and tongue and, after a varying period, perhaps a month, find their way to the stomach where they attach themselves to the lining. The bot larvae live only in horses.

The larvae remain for about a year and then pass through the intestines to the outside in the faeces. They emerge in the spring and, after several weeks of further development on the ground, hatch into flies. The bot upsets the horse considerably and may cause it to gallop about in attempts to get away. As the laying of the eggs does not actually hurt, there would seem to be an instinctive knowledge of the harm the larvae can do once they gain entrance to the body. While attached to the stomach wall the larvae produce a ring-like thickening in the lining. Large numbers may accumulate and cause irritation and even perforation of the bowel. The side effects produced by the larvae include loss of condition, and some claim that crib biting may result from their presence in the pharynx.

Some people attach little significance to the bot, while others go to great lengths to protect and treat their horses. Bot flies have been practically eliminated by the regular use of Ivermectin which kills both flies and their maggots.

The bot and the warble should not be confused with the horse fly, which is a large, robust fly with prominent eyes. The horse fly lays its eggs on the leaves of plants and the larvae develop, not in animals, but in mud or water. The flies are seen in summer, especially in thundery weather. They attach themselves to horses and cattle, feeding by biting and sucking blood. The bites are painful and irritate sensitive skinned animals, giving rise to swelling or weals. There seems to be no immediate prospect of ridding the world of flies, even with the extensive use of modern chemicals such as Ivermectin, DDT, Gammexane and so on which kill insects so effectively. The time when the warble fly and its maggot are eliminated forever should not, however, be far distant.

Red worm

What might a foal that drops dead, a yearling that dies after a bout of colic and a horse in training which fails to thrive or lacks stamina have in common? Each could be the result of red worm infection, a serious problem to the thoroughbred industry.

This threat to the health of thoroughbred horses has been known for a long time. Its effects have certainly been reduced in recent years by modern methods of control, but it is important to remember that this potential enemy is ever present and its consequences are all too often seen every day.

The red worm is a very small parasite measuring only 15-45mm in length. Its colour is not naturally red, but is due to the horse's blood on which it feeds while it is present in the gut. There are many different types of red worm, for which the family name is *strongylidae*. The one that causes the most damage is known as *strongylus vulgaris*.

The grown worms live in the large intestine of the horse and the females lay eggs which are passed in the faeces. From the eggs they hatch into the young stage known as larvae. The larvae crawl on to the grass and are here picked up by other horses grazing in the paddock. Once the larvae have been swallowed, they pass with the food into the small intestine and here burrow into the wall of the gut, entering the blood vessels. In the blood vessels, the larvae travel towards the main blood vessel of the body known as the aorta. During this time they feed and develop until ready to return to the gut as adults. It is unusual for them to go further than the point where the arteries to the gut leave the aorta, although occasionally they may be carried to more distant parts of the body such as the heart, lungs and kidney.

Once they have returned to the gut, the females start to lay eggs and the life cycle is complete. The length of time between the swallowing of the young larvae from the grass to the time that the adult stage is reached is about four months.

The fact that S *vulgaris* is the red worm whose young form lives in the bloodstream makes it the most dangerous horse parasite found in this country. Other types of red worm spend their life within the horse inside the gut and their larvae do not enter the bloodstream. While they may cause serious local damage, the overall effect is usually not nearly so serious as S *vulgaris*.

When the larvae travel in the blood vessels they injure the walls causing their normally smooth surface to become rough. The damage may be so great that the elastic nature of the wall is destroyed and large cavities, known as aneurysms, form. This is most likely to occur at the point where the artery to the small gut leaves the aorta. These cavities become filled with blood clot and in this way the supply of blood to a large length of gut may become restricted or even completely cut-off. The normal digestion of the horse may also suffer and in consequence the animal may be permanently unthrifty, or his stamina may be impaired without a marked loss in condition. If the damage to the wall of the blood vessel extends through all its layers a rupture may occur and the animal die suddenly from internal haemorrhage. This disaster is most commonly seen in foals and yearlings.

The adult strongyles live in the gut. If they are present in large numbers they may cause ulceration and irritation of the bowel resulting in diarrhoea, loss of condition and anaemia.

The economic effect of these parasites is much greater than the loss from sudden death or obvious clinical symptoms would suggest. A purchaser of a yearling may quite unsuspectingly be paying for an animal which has already been seriously affected by red worms, and yet show no outward indication of how much damage has been caused to the blood vessels inside the body. It is the young horses which suffer the most serious damage in the blood vessels. Infection with S vulgaris after the age of two or three years becomes progressively less dangerous and quite large numbers of worms may then be carried in the gut without any serious results to the individual itself. As the animal becomes older it may gain an immunity or tolerance which is certainly not possessed by yearlings and foals. It is therefore obviously necessary to see that the young thoroughbred is given as little opportunity as possible to eat the red worm larvae.

The larvae are picked up in the paddocks where the foals and yearlings graze. Larvae are put there in the droppings of the mares and other horses which may graze there. The mother of a foal may be putting on the pastures many hundreds of thousands of larvae a day, some of which may be consumed by her own foal. In this way, all her efforts in carrying and rearing the foal may be set at nought.

It might be thought that the loosebox would be a ready source of S vulgaris larvae but, fortunately, the larvae must crawl on to the grass before they become infective. The conditions in the loosebox do not allow them to develop.

There are a number of ways in which the risk of the larvae being eaten by the young stock on the pastures can be reduced. By regular treatment with certain drugs of all animals over the age of 6 months, it is possible to reduce the number of red worm eggs being passed in the faeces to practically zero. The drugs in common use today are the benzamidazole group and Ivermectin. The benzamidazoles are least expensive but do not affect the young larval forms of red worm which are migrating through blood vessels. These compounds are very safe and cause no harm to any class of animals to which they are given in the correct doses. Their effect is to kill the worms in the gut or to prevent the females from laying eggs. For two reasons they must, however, be given regularly throughout the year. In the first case, they kill only the adult worms in the gut and not the larvae in the blood vessels. There is, therefore, ample opportunity for the larvae to leave the blood vessels and grow into adults in the gut when the effects of the drug have worn off. There is, so to speak, a reservoir of young worms which only seem to leave their hideouts in the bloodstream when the number of adults in the gut are reduced. The second reason which makes regular treatment necessary is the continual possibility of reinfection by the animal picking up larvae from the pasture.

There are many different systems of regular dosing, some with small doses daily, others with larger doses weekly or monthly. The results of these different systems are the same, but in order to check the dropping of egg-laden dungs on the pasture is successfully being prevented, regular examinations of the faeces can be made. In these examinations, a small portion is examined under a microscope and the number of eggs counted. It is common to express these results as the number of eggs per gramme. It must be remembered, however, that a count of 200 eggs per gramme means that many hundreds of thousands of eggs may be dropped by that animal in one dung. The count of eggs in any one individual cannot be taken as conclusive proof of the levels of infection within an animal, as a few females may be laying a

Parasites

large number of eggs. Nor, of course, do they indicate the damage done by the larvae before they become adults and lay the eggs that are being counted. Only a small proportion of one dung is being examined and an infinitesimal portion of the total droppings during the day. It is to be expected, therefore, that the counts will vary even in one dung although, if the methods used are accurate, the variation should only be in the order of 200-300 eggs per gramme at the most.

On the studs, regular examinations of the faeces in this manner is advisable even though treatment is being carried out. The results then give an overall picture of the position in all the animals present on the stud and it is thus possible to gauge the efficiency of the preventive measures. Horses in training that have no access to pasture can still give high counts in the faeces because of the continual passage of larvae from the bloodstream into the gut. Continuous treatment will eventually reduce the numbers in the animals' bodies to very low levels. The result of damage to the blood vessels in early life by the migrating larvae may, however, already have left a permanent scar which no treatment can remedy.

For practical purposes, it is most important to concentrate control measures on the animals that are grazing in the paddocks where foals and yearlings are kept. It is particularly important, therefore, to treat and to do faecal counts on in-foal mares, mares with foals at foot and yearlings, as opposed to barren mares living in the outlying paddocks, although the latter must not be neglected. Because no means of treatment is likely to be 100 per cent effective in preventing the passing of eggs, the regular picking up of dungs from the pastures is still one of the most important jobs on a stud. The dungs have to be removed within 24-48 hours after dropping for the system to be fully effective, as the larvae migrate away into the pasture fairly quickly. This second line of defence provided by the removal of dungs also aids the pasture growth, as horse dung tends to sour the grass. A third method of reducing the number of larvae on the paddock is to keep horses off the pasture for several months.

The length of life of the larvae on the pasture varies with the conditions, being shortened by dry weather and sun, and increased by moisture and shade. There will, however, be steady reduction in their numbers as each month goes by and 6 months rest without the addition of new material is a very good practical time.

The development of a vaccine which would prevent the larvae from entering the bloodstream would seem to be the only conclusive method of eliminating the dangers of red worm infestation in this country, where pastures are used continually for the grazing of thoroughbreds. Ivermectin has dramatically altered the situation of worm control in recent years. This compound kills not only worms in the gut but also young larval forms as they migrate through the blood vessels and tissues. Its regular use (usually recommended every 6 weeks) can virtually keep young horses free of adult and young larval parasites.